Ball® CANNING
BACK TO BASICS

A FOOLPROOF GUIDE TO CANNING JAMS, JELLIES, PICKLES & MORE

Oxmoor House®

Published by Oxmoor House, an imprint of Time Inc. Books
225 Liberty Street, New York, NY 10281

Culinary Marketing Manager: Sarah Green Page
Senior Editor: Betty Wong
Senior Manager, Business Development + Partnerships: Nina Reed
Project Editor: Lacie Pinyan
Design Director: Melissa Clark
Photo Director: Paden Reich
Photographers: Caitlin Bensel, Monica Buck, Hélène Dujardin, Alison Miksch,
Whitney Ott, Victor Protasio, Hector Manuel Sanchez
Prop Stylists: Mary Clayton Carl, Kay E. Clarke, Missie Neville Crawford,
Audrey Davis, Thom Driver, Mindi Shapiro Levine, Lindsey Lower, Claire Spollen
Food Stylists: Mary Claire Britton, Torie Cox, Katelyn Hardwick,
Rishon Hanners, Tina Stamos
Prop Coordinator: Audrey Davis
Senior Production Manager: Greg A. Amason
Assistant Production Director: Sue Chodakiewicz
Copy Writer: Julie Christopher
Copy Editor: Donna Baldone
Proofreader: Jacqueline Giovanelli
Quality Assurance Engineer: Matt Cheever
Indexer: Mary Ann Laurens

Special Thanks: Chris Carlisle, Matt Christensen, Janine Moore

ISBN-13: 978-0-8487-5452-5
Library of Congress Control Number: 2017937388

First Edition 2017

Printed in the United States of America

10 9 8 7 6 5 4 3

We welcome your comments and suggestions about Time Inc. Books.
Time Inc. Books
Attention: Book Editors
P.O. Box 62310
Tampa, Florida 33662-2310

Time Inc. Books products may be purchased for business or promotional use.
For information on bulk purchases, please contact Christi Crowley in the
Special Sales Department at (845) 895-9858.

CONTENTS

INTRODUCTION

Welcome to *Ball Canning Back to Basics*! We're super excited to share this compilation of 100 favorite and most requested water bath canning recipes with you. We hope that it will make capturing the sweet, ripe flavors of summer easier than ever. Whether you're using fruit you've picked yourself for a simple berry jam or looking for the perfect pickle recipe for those beautiful farmers' market cucumbers or chile peppers, you'll find everything you need right here, simplified and illustrated with photos to inform and demystify every step along the way. We heard a desire from many of you for a collection of straightforward, simple, and classic recipes, all in one place; so here they are.

We have been the canning experts for over 100 years and we are just as dedicated today to your preserving success as we were back then, before there were supermarkets and every jar was precious. Here at The Fresh Preserving Test Kitchen, we know that every jar is still precious, that's why we thoroughly test and stand behind all the recipes we create. Our quality engineers work hand in hand with our culinary team to ensure every recipe works, tastes great, and most important, is totally safe for pantry storage. Each recipe is tested for pH, viscosity, thermal penetration, and water activity. These results are then adjusted as needed to create a perfect balance of time, temperature, and ingredients to ensure the results are both as safe and delicious as possible.

It is also our goal to make your fresh preserving experience as simple and fun as possible, even if you've never canned before. It's for this reason that this back to basics book focuses on the water bath canning method of preservation and features quick-cook recipes. Water bath canning doesn't require special equipment and is the simplest technique for the home cook to master. With very few exceptions, the soft spread recipes in this book make use of all natural Ball® Pectin to assure a perfect set every time, but in a fraction of the time it takes for a traditional long-cook recipe. As a result, the super-fresh fruit flavor really shines through.

As for pickles, we've included two simple and classic fermented pickle recipes as an introduction to traditional pickle making. The remainder are super-easy fresh-pack pickles of all kinds to fill your shelves with crunchy, tangy vegetables year-round. We even have some pantry staple recipes, such as Saucy Sloppy Joe Starter (page 154) and Ketchup (page 137) to make use of your kitchen garden tomato crop.

Canning your own food is truly a balance of art and science, one that fosters a reconnection with what's important, whether it is time spent with family and friends in the kitchen or the satisfaction of cooking up something special that speaks to your sense of creativity and self-sufficiency. It's also a way to take back control of your pantry. You can feel good knowing exactly what's in every jar, because you picked it, cooked it, and canned it yourself. Whether your inspiration is in the creation or the preservation, the result is always pure and authentic.

Enjoy and let us know what you think at www.freshpreserving.com. We're here to help.

Sarah Green Page
Chef and Culinary Marketing Manager
The Fresh Preserving Test Kitchen

PRESERVING 101: WATER BATH CANNING

Water bath canning is a simple preservation method used only for high-acid or acidulated foods, fruits to pickles, that creates an anaerobic environment in a vacuum-sealed jar. This high-acid environment is inhospitable to molds, yeasts, bacteria, and enzymes (the spoilers).

HERE'S HOW IT WORKS

A sealed jar filled with food is submerged in a bath of boiling water long enough to bring the food inside to 212°F. The heat expands the food, pushing out all the air. When the jar is removed from the water bath, it begins to cool and contract, which forms the vacuum seal (and the famous "pinging" sound Ball® canning lids make). This newly created sealed environment is what makes the contents safe for long-term room temperature storage. It keeps any harmful microorganisms out while killing off any remaining in the food.

THE IMPORTANCE OF ACIDITY

The most important factor in determining how to safely preserve foods for pantry storage is acidity—the pH level of the food (or recipe). The lower the pH, the higher the acidity. Foods having naturally high levels of acid, or those with a sufficient amount of acid added to decrease the pH level to 4.6 or lower, may be processed in a boiling water canner. As the chart on page 9 shows, fruits are naturally high in acid, while vegetables are not. While fruits, jams, and jellies are generally classified as high-acid foods, some fruits, such as figs, rhubarb, papaya, melons,

and tomatoes require the addition of extra acid, commonly citric acid from lemon or lime juice. This will ensure that a safe pH is maintained throughout and after processing. Mixing high-acid foods with low-acid foods in a recipe requires acidulation. With salsas and chutneys, for instance, the low-acid foods can raise the pH level and cause dangerous conditions once canned, which is why it is necessary to follow thoroughly tested recipes and the safe processing times indicated.

NOTE: The use of fresh lemon or lime juice in some of the recipes in this book is done for the purpose of fresh flavor. Be assured that any recipe that calls for fresh lemon or lime juice has been thoroughly verified as safe by scientific testing.

FRUITS AND SOFT SPREADS

You need four key ingredients to make jams, jellies, preserves, and marmalades successfully: fruit, acid, pectin, and sugar. A balance of all four of these ingredients is necessary to achieve a successful set (or gel).

SUGAR has preserving properties, as it replaces some of the water in the fruit, helping jams and jellies set and become glossy. It also helps preserve color during storage and delay spoiling by microorganisms and enzymes once jars are opened. Low-sugar/no-sugar fruit jams and jellies preserve just as safely but need to be consumed quickly once opened.

PECTIN is a natural substance found in fruits, vegetables, and plants that is responsible for cell structure. It is needed in soft spreads to thicken and bind the fruit and juices together. The traditional method of making jams does not use added pectin but requires long cooking before the fruit breaks down enough to thicken and set. (To know when your long-cook recipe is done, refer to Testing the Set or Gel on page 18.)

Quick-cook recipes use added pectin to help the spread set properly so you can spend less time at the stove. Commercial pectin, such as Ball® RealFruit® Classic Pectin, Ball® RealFruit® Low or No-Sugar Needed Pectin, Ball® RealFruit® Instant Pectin, and Ball® RealFruit® Liquid Pectin, is extracted from fruits that have very naturally high levels of pectin. The recipes in this book give complete instructions for the type of pectin to be used, as well as the correct balance of acid, fruit, and sugar needed to achieve a satisfactory set. Each type of pectin has unique attributes and therefore are not interchangeable.

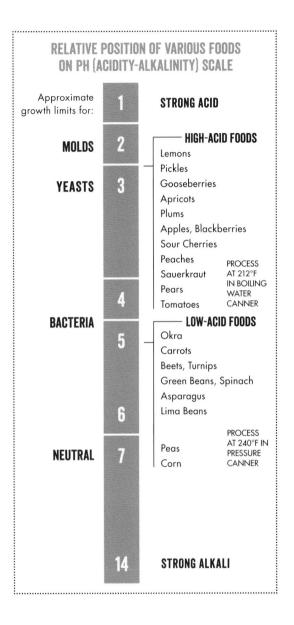

RELATIVE POSITION OF VARIOUS FOODS ON PH (ACIDITY-ALKALINITY) SCALE

Approximate growth limits for:

1 — STRONG ACID

MOLDS — 2 — HIGH-ACID FOODS
Lemons
Pickles

YEASTS — 3 — Gooseberries
Apricots
Plums
Apples, Blackberries
Sour Cherries
Peaches — PROCESS AT 212°F IN BOILING WATER CANNER
Sauerkraut
Pears
4 — Tomatoes

BACTERIA — LOW-ACID FOODS
5 — Okra
Carrots
Beets, Turnips
Green Beans, Spinach
Asparagus
Lima Beans
6

7 — Peas — PROCESS AT 240°F IN PRESSURE CANNER
NEUTRAL — Corn

14 — STRONG ALKALI

JELLY

MARMALADE

FRUIT

PRESERVES

JAM

KNOW YOUR TERMS

JAM Thick, firm spread made by cooking crushed or chopped fruit and sugar to the gelling point.

JELLY A shimmery, translucent spread made using juice extracted from fruits or vegetables.

PRESERVES This spread is made with large uniform pieces of fruit cooked with sugar. The texture can vary from thick syrup to a very soft jelly.

MARMALADE The addition of small pieces of fruit and peel differentiates marmalades from jellies and jams. Marmalades are commonly made from citrus fruits, either on their own or paired with other fruits and vegetables. Citrus fruits have great quantities of natural pectin that is contained in the albedo, or pith, part of the peel (the white flesh between the peel and the fruit itself).

FRUIT IN SYRUP Whole, halved, or sliced fruits are preserved in sugar syrup, juice, or water. The sugar syrup helps fruit retain a bright color, firm texture, and flavor.

FRUIT BUTTER A thick, smooth spread made of pureed fruit and sugar. Spices or a second fruit or fruit juice may be added for flavor.

CANNING TOMATOES

Tomatoes are the glorious fruit we use as a vegetable. They are in the danger range on the pH scale, as some varieties are sweet and contain less acid. Some, notably heirloom, tomatoes are 4.6 pH or higher, and as they ripen their pH level rises even higher, which makes it necessary to add acid during canning to ensure a safe pH is maintained. Citric acid, lemon or lime juice, and vinegar have low pH and bring different flavors to tomato recipes. A pinch of sugar can offset the tartness.

Canning tomatoes whole, halved, or quartered can be done by either of two methods: raw pack or hot pack. Raw pack refers to raw, peeled tomatoes packed into jars, and then topped off with hot water. With the hot-pack method, the tomatoes are heated through, and then packed into jars and topped off with the hot cooking liquid. Citric acid or lemon juice is always added, along with desired dry seasonings. The recipes in this book give you the option to use either Ball® Citric Acid or lemon juice to ensure a safe pH. The tomato-based salsas included in the book are loaded with fresh vegetables like onions and chiles and have plenty of added acid, making them safe for water bath preservation.

PICKLING

Pickling is so much more than just cucumbers in a salty vinegar brine. It's the process of preserving vegetables and fruits in vinegar or with salt by fermentation (which is a whole other book!). Both vinegar and salt have preserving qualities: Salt draws out water from produce, helping it stay crunchy, while vinegar adds the acid needed to help keep preserved vegetables safe to eat. Together with herbs and spices, vinegar and salt create that distinctly tangy "pickled" flavor that can be sweet, spicy, or full of garlic and dill.

When pickling, for best results use only granulated salt with no additives, such as Ball® Salt for Pickling and Preserving. Different vinegars offer unique flavoring options; just be sure the one you're using has 5% acidity. Anything less than 5% acidity can cause the pH of your pickle to be thrown out of balance, making the pickle potentially unsafe. Pickle brine contains water. Avoid using hard water since it has minerals that can have an adverse effect on your final pickle. Instead, use soft, spring, or distilled water. A great way to ensure extra crispness when making fresh-pack pickles is to use a crisping agent, such as Ball® Pickle Crisp® Granules (calcium chloride, a naturally occurring salt found in some mineral deposits).

In this book, we include recipes for fresh pack and refrigerator pickles, relishes, and chutneys. Fresh and refrigerator pickles are fresh-pack, meaning the produce is put into jars either raw or quickly heated, usually along with the spices, and then a hot vinegar brine is poured over the pickles, which then can be either preserved in a water bath canner for shelf storage in the pantry, or put in the refrigerator for convenient quick eating. Relish is basically a pickle with ingredients that have been diced or chopped. It's usually cooked in its brine, which will be thick, before ladling into jars. Chutney refers to a type of relish that usually contains a combination of fruit, vinegar, sugar, and spices, originating from South Asia.

As a general rule, keep freshly harvested vegetables very cold and use them within 24 hours. Although they are safe to eat immediately, pickles will develop a uniform flavor and texture if allowed to stand for 3 weeks in the refrigerator after processing in jars.

1

6

5

4

2

3

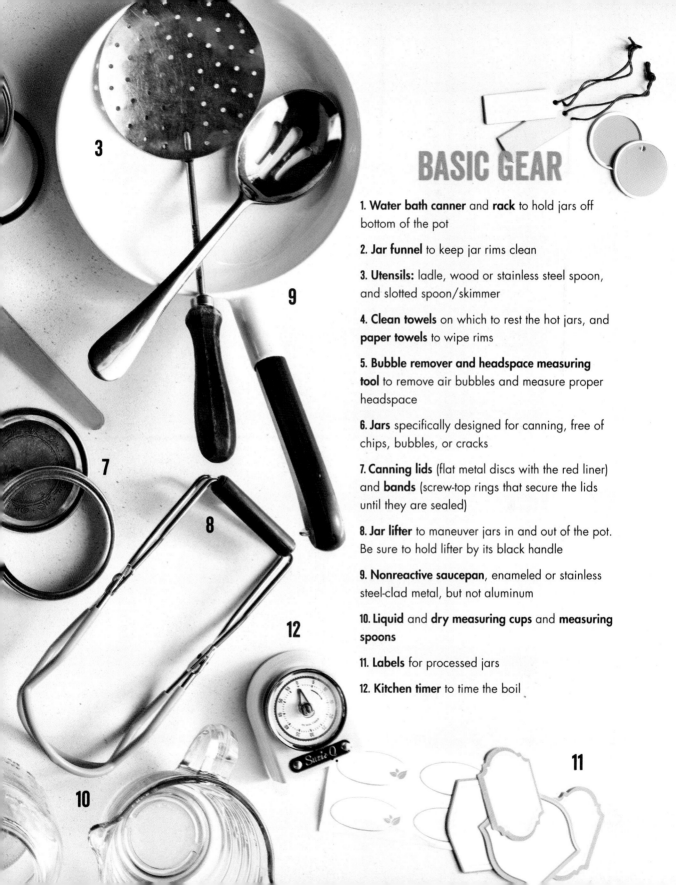

BASIC GEAR

1. **Water bath canner** and **rack** to hold jars off bottom of the pot

2. **Jar funnel** to keep jar rims clean

3. **Utensils:** ladle, wood or stainless steel spoon, and slotted spoon/skimmer

4. **Clean towels** on which to rest the hot jars, and **paper towels** to wipe rims

5. **Bubble remover and headspace measuring tool** to remove air bubbles and measure proper headspace

6. **Jars** specifically designed for canning, free of chips, bubbles, or cracks

7. **Canning lids** (flat metal discs with the red liner) and **bands** (screw-top rings that secure the lids until they are sealed)

8. **Jar lifter** to maneuver jars in and out of the pot. Be sure to hold lifter by its black handle

9. **Nonreactive saucepan**, enameled or stainless steel-clad metal, but not aluminum

10. **Liquid** and **dry measuring cups** and **measuring spoons**

11. **Labels** for processed jars

12. **Kitchen timer** to time the boil

CHOOSING THE RIGHT JARS

Water bath canning does not require special equipment, except for canning jars.

JAR SIZE Choose from over six jar sizes. Some jars have shoulders while others have straight sides that work best for freezing. (Only use straight-sided jars for freezing.) Your recipe will guide you on the recommended jar sizes. See the chart below for some suggestions to get you started.

MOUTH SIZE The diameter of the jar opening determines the mouth size. Choose from either regular or wide mouth sizes. All jelly jars have a regular mouth.

REGULAR MOUTH works best with pourable foods, such as jams, jellies, salsas, sauces, and pie fillings, or chopped fruits and vegetables.

WIDE MOUTH works best with whole fruits and vegetables or when you need a large mouth for filling.

	BALL® JAR SIZE	IDEAL FOR	FREEZER SAFE
REGULAR MOUTH	Jelly Jars (4 ounces)	Jams, jellies, mustards, ketchups, dipping sauces, flavored vinegars, and small portion sizes	❄
	Jelly Jars (8 ounces)	Jams, jellies, conserves, and preserves	❄
	Jelly Jars (12 ounces)	Jams, jellies, conserves, and marmalades	❄
	Half-Pint (8 ounces)	Fruit syrups, chutneys, and pizza sauces	❄
	Pint (16 ounces)	Salsas, sauces, relishes, and pie fillings	
	Quart (32 ounces)	Sliced fruits and vegetables, pickles, tomato-based juices, and sauces	
		IDEAL FOR	
WIDE MOUTH	Pint (16 ounces)	Salsas, sauces, relishes, and fruit butters	❄
	Pint & Half (24 ounces)	Asparagus, pickles, sauces, soups, and stews	❄
	Quart (32 ounces)	Pickles, tomatoes, and whole or halved fruits and vegetables	
	Half Gallon (64 ounces)	Apple and grape juices	

NOTE: When filling freezer-safe jars, leave ½-inch headspace to allow for food expansion during freezing.

GETTING STARTED

There are just a few simple steps to follow when water bath canning: prepare ingredients, cook recipe, fill jars, and process jars in a canner. But here are some important things to keep in mind to make sure your efforts are successful.

START WITH A GOOD RECIPE

Home canning does not require any special culinary skills, but factors like jar size, accurate measurements, specific ingredient preparation, and processing times all can affect the temperature and acidity of home canned foods. Be sure to use only reliable recipes that have been tested for home canning to ensure safe, nutritious results.

Begin by reading the recipe all the way through before you start. Set aside enough time to prepare and process the recipe without interruption. Each recipe will give specific instructions for coring, peeling, chopping, crushing, or juicing fruits and vegetables. Follow the preparation instructions carefully to ensure that the correct measure of produce is incorporated into the recipe for correct balance of ingredients. The recipe will also indicate if the ingredients need to be raw or cooked, and how much headspace to leave once you fill a jar.

KEEP IT CLEAN

Wash jars, lids, and bands. Before adding lids (always use new lids) and bands to your filled jar, make sure to clean the rim of the jar of any drips. Food residue can prevent the lid from sealing properly. Wipe the jars clean again before storing.

MEASURE HEADSPACE

Headspace is the unfilled space in the jar between the food or liquid and the rim of the jar. Each individual recipe will specify the correct headspace to use. Too much or too little space can prevent the lid from sealing properly. As a general rule, leave ¼-inch headspace for fruit juices, jams, jellies, and other soft spreads; ½-inch headspace for high-acid foods like fruits, tomatoes, and pickles.

TEST THE SEAL

After the processed jars have cooled and before you store them, test the lids to determine that they are vacuum sealed. Press the center of the lid to determine if it is concave. Remove the band and gently try to remove the lid with your fingertips. If the lid is concave and cannot be removed with your fingertips, the jar is vacuum sealed.

KNOW YOUR ALTITUDE

Barometric pressure is reduced at high altitudes, affecting the temperature at which water boils. This means boiling water and pressure processing methods must be adjusted to ensure the safety of home-canned food. Additional processing time must be added when using the boiling water method. The altitude chart below gives adjustments for various elevations.

Processing times and temperatures for recipes in this book are based on canning at an elevation of 1,000 feet above sea level or lower. If you are processing at a higher elevation, refer to the altitude chart for adjustments.

Contact your Natural Resources Conservation Service, Cooperative Extension Service, or Public Library Service for the altitude in your area.

BOILING WATER CANNER ALTITUDE ADJUSTMENTS

ALTITUDE IN FEET	INCREASE PROCESSING TIME
1,001 to 3,000	5 minutes
3,001 to 6,000	10 minutes
6,001 to 8,000	15 minutes
8,001 to 10,000	20 minutes

STORE SAFELY

Home-canned foods may be safely stored without bands. Label sealed jars with the recipe name and processing date. Store jars in a cool (50° to 70°F), dry, dark place for up to a year. Once you open a jar, keep it in the refrigerator for up to 3 weeks, or 3 months for pickles.

Testing the Set or Gel

Jams, jellies, and marmalades are all about the gelling action. Getting your preserves to "set" when using added pectin is easy, but achieving the perfect gel point when making traditional no-pectin-added preserves just takes a few extra steps.

Follow these easy tests to know when your spread is perfect. Remove your pot from the burner while testing. If after testing you find your recipe isn't ready, turn your pot to high heat and boil for only a few minutes more before retesting.

TEMPERATURE TEST
The temperature test can be used for all soft spreads. Set a candy thermometer on the edge of your jam pot making sure it does not touch the sides or bottom. Once the preserve is at a rolling boil, start monitoring the temperature. Gel is achieved once the thermometer reads 220°F (at 1,000 feet) or 8°F above boiling point for your elevation.

FROZEN PLATE OR SPOON TEST
The frozen plate or spoon test can also be used to test all spreads. Place several small plates or several spoons in the freezer. As your preserve begins to boil down and thicken, take a plate or spoon out, and use your jam stirring spoon to scoop a small amount onto the frozen plate. Return plate to freezer for a few minutes. The jam is set if it wrinkles when pushed with your finger and does not have a pool of syrup around it.

SPOON TEST
The sheet test or "sheeting" is used primarily for jelly and marmalades along with the temperature test: Dip a large metal spoon into the boiling jelly, lift it out, and hold it horizontally over the pot letting the jelly slide off. When drops come together along the edge of the spoon forming a thick sheet, the preserve is ready. If the drops are light and syrupy, it's not ready. Continue to boil for a few minutes more and retest.

WHAT TO KNOW ABOUT SPOILAGE
Before you can fully understand how food is safely preserved for pantry storage during the home-canning process, it is helpful to become familiar with how and why food spoils in the first place and how spoilage can be prevented.

MOLDS AND YEAST Molds are visible and nonvisible fungi that grow in food. Although some mold is relatively harmless, certain molds can produce mycotoxins that are toxic. Yeasts are also a form of fungi that cause fermentation. Both can make for inedible food that may even be harmful to eat. Foods of low pH are largely protected from bacterial growth; however, molds and yeasts are ever-present and, if left untreated, continue to grow. But don't worry, they are easily destroyed when exposed to high temperatures (between 140° and 190°F. Since boiling water canners heat food to 212°F, high-acid foods can safely be preserved using this method.

BACTERIA Bacteria are not easily destroyed by heat; in fact, certain bacteria actually thrive at temperatures that destroy molds and yeasts and will continue to survive in the absence of oxygen within a moist environment—exactly the conditions inside a sealed jar of food. As all of the canning recipes in this book have a pH that is well below 4.6, processing the jars using a water bath is sufficient for ensuring a safe result. Sweet, ripe tomatoes, as noted earlier, have a pH that is borderline for water bath processing but the addition of citric acid or lemon juice in our recipes ensures a safe pH is maintained.

ENZYMES Enzymes are proteins that are present in all living things and are the catalysts that promote organic changes and reactions in our bodies and in food. They promote spoilage if not inactivated. Luckily, enzymes are easily inactivated by temperatures starting at 140°F. Therefore, they are easily inactivated in a boiling water process.

SIGNS OF SPOILAGE

Do not taste food from a jar that comes unsealed or shows signs of spoilage. Examine each jar of food carefully before using it to ensure a vacuum seal is present. Lids that are concave indicate the jar is sealed. Do not use any jar of food that is unsealed, has a bulging lid, or does not require a can opener for the lid to be removed.

Food spoilage produces gases that cause the lids to swell and/or break their seals. Visually

---

INDICATIONS THAT THE FOOD HAS SPOILED INCLUDE:

- Broken seal
- Mold
- Gassiness
- Cloudiness
- Spurting liquid
- Bubbles rising in jar
- Seepage
- Yeast growth
- Fermentation
- Slime
- Unpleasant odor

---

examine jars of food for other signs of spoilage that might be present. Jars that are suspected of containing spoiled low-acid or tomato products must be handled carefully. They may exhibit different signs of spoilage or no signs of spoilage. If you suspect your jar contains spoiled food, handle carefully. Place jars of sealed home-canned food showing signs of spoilage in a garbage bag. Secure the bag closed and place it in the regular trash container or dispose of it at a landfill.

Home-canned food that shows signs of spoilage must be discarded in a manner that ensures no human or animal will come in contact with the product. Contact with botulinum toxin can be fatal whether it is ingested or enters the body through the skin. Avoid contact with suspect food.

1

JAMS, PRESERVES, and MARMALADES

These are some of the most iconic and versatile spreads you can make. Quick-cook jams offer bright fruit color and flavor—best of all, they require only four ingredients: crushed fruit, sugar, acid, and pectin. Preserves, made with large pieces of fruit, are cooked so the fruit becomes tender and develops a glossy, transparent appearance. Marmalades are sweet-tart spreads with small pieces of fruit and peel.

HOW TO MAKE JAMS, PRESERVES, and MARMALADES

You will need:

- Tested recipe and ingredients
- Glass preserving jars with lids and bands (always start with new lids)
- Water bath canner or a large, deep stockpot with lid and rack
- Jar lifter
- Common kitchen utensils, including measuring cups and spoons, large ladle, kitchen towel, and rubber spatula
- Large stainless-steel or enameled saucepan or Dutch oven
- Canning funnel
- Bubble remover and headspace measuring tool
- Labels

TIPS

You may also use a dishwasher to wash and heat the jars.

To ensure a correct pH and balanced flavor, prepare all the recipes as written. Substituting ingredients, doubling, or changing the recipe measurements may result in an unsuccessful set or spoilage on the pantry shelf.

To reduce foam in step 4, you can add ½ teaspoon butter or margarine after removing the saucepan from the heat, stirring to blend well.

STEP 1: HEAT JARS Examine the jars for defects. Place a canning rack at the bottom of the canner and fill halfway with water. Place the jars in the water and bring almost to a simmer over medium. **IMPORTANT:** Keep the jars hot until ready to fill to prevent jar breakage due to thermal shock. Wash the lids and bands in warm soapy water, rinse, and set aside.

STEP 2: PREP INGREDIENTS Prepare the ingredients according to the recipe. Rinse fruit under cold running water instead of soaking it so it doesn't absorb moisture. Crush the fruit if noted in the recipe.

STEP 3: COOK Combine the prepared fruit and other ingredients noted in the recipe in a large stainless-steel or enameled saucepan or Dutch oven. Cook as directed in the recipe.

STEP 4: Add the sugar or other sweetener, stirring to dissolve. (Note: If your recipe calls for Ball® Liquid Pectin, add at this stage.) Return to a full rolling boil. Boil hard 1 minute, stirring constantly. Remove from heat. Skim the foam.

STEP 5: FILL Using a ladle and canning funnel, fill a hot jar with the hot jam, preserves, or marmalade, leaving ¼-inch headspace. Remove air bubbles. Wipe the rim and top of the jar with a clean, damp cloth to remove any food residue, which can prevent a vacuum seal.

STEP 6: Center the lid on the jar, allowing sealing compound to come in contact with the jar rim. Apply the band and adjust until fit is fingertip-tight. Make sure the band is not overtightened—air inside the jars must be able to escape during canning.

STEP 7: Place the filled jar in the canner. Repeat one at a time until all the jars are filled. (If using a canning rack, lower the rack with the jars into the water.) Make sure the water covers the jars by at least 1 inch. Add more hot water if needed.

STEP 8: PROCESS Place the lid on the canner and bring water to a full rolling boil. Once the water is fully boiling, start timing for the length of time stated in the recipe (adjusting for altitude, see page 16). Maintain a rolling boil throughout the entire processing period. After processing time is complete, turn off the heat and remove lid. Let the canner cool 5 minutes before removing the jars.

STEP 9: Using the jar lifter, remove the jars from the canner and set upright on a towel or cutting board, leaving at least 2 inches between the jars. Leave undisturbed for at least 12 hours. The bands may loosen during processing but should not be retightened, as this may interfere with the sealing process.

STEP 10: TEST & STORE Check the lids for vacuum seals after stand time. Lids should not flex up and down when the center is pressed. Remove the bands. Gently try to lift off the lids with your fingertips. If the lid cannot be lifted off, the lid has a good seal. Wipe the jars and the lids with a clean, damp cloth. Label and store in a cool, dry, dark place up to 1 year.

JAMS, PRESERVES, and MARMALADES

SOUR CHERRY JAM

MAKES ABOUT 4 (½-PINT) JARS

This tart cherry jam is glorious as a filling for crêpes or as a topping on ricotta crostini or mini cheesecakes. If you can't find fresh fruit, you can also use frozen cherries.

❶ Combine the cherries and the pectin in a 6-quart stainless-steel or enameled Dutch oven. Bring the mixture to a full rolling boil that cannot be stirred down, over high, stirring constantly.

❷ Add the sugar, stirring to dissolve. Return to a full rolling boil. Boil hard 1 minute, stirring constantly. Remove from heat. Skim the foam, if necessary.

❸ Ladle the hot jam into a hot jar, leaving ¼-inch headspace. Wipe the jar rim. Center the lid on the jar. Apply the band, and adjust to fingertip-tight. Place the jar in the boiling water canner. Repeat until all the jars are filled.

❹ Process the jars 10 minutes, adjusting for altitude. Turn off heat; remove the lid, and let the jars stand 5 minutes. Remove the jars and cool.

CHANGE IT UP

Make a bigger batch. For 6 (½-pint) jars, start with 4 cups chopped cherries, 4½ tablespoons Ball® Classic Pectin, and 5 cups sugar. Or consult the Pectin Calculator at www.freshpreserving.com for the amount desired.

2⅔ cups fresh or frozen chopped pitted tart red cherries

3 tablespoons Ball® Classic Pectin

3⅓ cups sugar

LOW SUGAR

Add ⅔ cup unsweetened fruit juice or water to the cherries and substitute 3 tablespoons Ball® Low or No-Sugar Needed Pectin for the Classic Pectin. Reduce the sugar to 1 cup. This jam will have a looser set than the full-sugar version, but just as much fresh fruit flavor.

SWEET CHERRY JAM

The hardest part of this recipe is pitting the cherries, but the effort is well worth it when the result is a beautiful, luscious spread that is stellar slathered on toast or paired with goat cheese.

2⅔ cups fresh or frozen chopped pitted dark sweet cherries

2 tablespoons lemon juice

3 tablespoons Ball® Classic Pectin

3⅓ cups sugar

LOW SUGAR

Add ⅔ cup unsweetened fruit juice or water to the cherries and lemon juice, substituting 3 tablespoons Ball® Low or No-Sugar Needed Pectin for the Classic Pectin. Reduce the sugar to 1 cup. This jam will have a looser set than the full-sugar version, but just as much fresh fruit flavor.

❶ Stir together the chopped cherries and the lemon juice in a 6-quart stainless-steel or enameled Dutch oven. Stir in the pectin. Bring the mixture to a full rolling boil that cannot be stirred down, over high, stirring constantly.

❷ Add the sugar, stirring to dissolve. Return to a full rolling boil. Boil hard 1 minute, stirring constantly. Remove from heat. Skim the foam, if necessary.

❸ Ladle the hot jam into a hot jar, leaving ¼-inch headspace. Wipe the jar rim. Center the lid on the jar. Apply the band, and adjust to fingertip-tight. Place the jar in the boiling water canner. Repeat until all the jars are filled.

❹ Process the jars 10 minutes, adjusting for altitude. Turn off heat; remove the lid, and let the jars stand 5 minutes. Remove the jars and cool.

APRICOT JAM

This versatile jam is a shortcut to glazes for chicken, pork, and shrimp, and makes an irresistible filling between white or yellow cake layers.

1 Combine the apricots and the pectin in a 6-quart stainless-steel or enameled Dutch oven. Bring the mixture to a full rolling boil that cannot be stirred down, over high, stirring constantly.

2 Add the sugar, stirring to dissolve. Return to a full rolling boil. Boil hard 1 minute, stirring constantly. Remove from heat. Skim the foam, if necessary.

3 Ladle the hot jam into a hot jar, leaving ¼-inch headspace. Wipe the jar rim. Center the lid on the jar. Apply the band, and adjust to fingertip-tight. Place the jar in the boiling water canner. Repeat until all the jars are filled.

4 Process the jars 10 minutes, adjusting for altitude. Turn off heat; remove the lid, and let the jars stand 5 minutes. Remove the jars and cool.

2⅔ cups finely chopped pitted apricots

3 tablespoons Ball® Classic Pectin

3⅓ cups sugar

LOW SUGAR

Add ⅔ cup unsweetened fruit juice or water to the apricots and substitute 3 tablespoons Ball® Low or No-Sugar Needed Pectin for the Classic Pectin. Reduce the sugar to 1 cup. This jam will have a looser set than the full-sugar version, but just as much fresh fruit flavor.

CHANGE IT UP

Make a super-easy Thai-inspired glaze. Combine a jar of apricot jam with grated ginger, cilantro, and a spoonful of sambal oelek chili sauce. Thin with rice vinegar or warm water. Brush over chicken, pork, or shrimp while grilling.

NECTARINE–SOUR CHERRY JAM

MAKES ABOUT 7 (½-PINT) JARS

**The tart acidic flavor of the cherries is terrific with this
sweet stone fruit. Choose firm, ripe, unblemished nectarines,
and keep them at cool room temperature before canning.**

1½ pounds nectarines, pitted and
finely chopped (about 5
nectarines)

2 cups chopped pitted fresh or
frozen tart red cherries

6 tablespoons Ball® Classic Pectin

2 tablespoons lemon juice

6 cups sugar

❶ Combine the first 4 ingredients in a 4-quart stainless-steel or
enameled Dutch oven. Bring the mixture to a full rolling boil that
cannot be stirred down, over high, stirring constantly.

❷ Add the sugar, stirring to dissolve. Return the mixture to a full
rolling boil. Boil hard 1 minute, stirring constantly. Remove from
heat. Skim the foam, if necessary.

❸ Ladle the hot jam into a hot jar, leaving ¼-inch headspace.
Wipe the jar rim. Center the lid on the jar. Apply the band, and
adjust to fingertip-tight. Place the jar in the boiling water canner.
Repeat until all the jars are filled.

❹ Process the jars 10 minutes, adjusting for altitude. Turn off heat;
remove the lid, and let the jars stand 5 minutes. Remove the jars
and cool.

CHANGE IT UP

Substitute blackberries, raspberries, blueberries, or
chopped strawberries in place of the sour cherries.

PLUM JAM

MAKES ABOUT 4 (½-PINT) JARS

Start with ripe, good-quality plums. Look for fruit with smooth skins and rich red-purple color.

2⅔ cups finely chopped pitted plums

3 tablespoons Ball® Classic Pectin

3⅓ cups sugar

LOW SUGAR

Add ⅔ cup unsweetened fruit juice or water to the plums and substitute 3 tablespoons Ball® Low or No-Sugar Needed Pectin for the Classic Pectin. Reduce the sugar to 1 cup. This jam will have a looser set than the full-sugar version, but just as much fresh fruit flavor.

❶ Combine the plums and the pectin in a 6-quart stainless-steel or enameled Dutch oven. Bring the mixture to a full rolling boil that cannot be stirred down, over high, stirring constantly.

❷ Add the sugar, stirring to dissolve. Return to a full rolling boil. Boil hard 1 minute, stirring constantly. Remove from heat. Skim the foam, if necessary.

❸ Ladle the hot jam into a hot jar, leaving ¼-inch headspace. Wipe the jar rim. Center the lid on the jar. Apply the band, and adjust to fingertip-tight. Place the jar in the boiling water canner. Repeat until all the jars are filled.

❹ Process the jars 10 minutes, adjusting for altitude. Turn off heat; remove the lid, and let the jars stand 5 minutes. Remove the jars and cool.

CHANGE IT UP

Make a quick-fix Asian barbecue sauce. Combine ½ cup jam with 1 tablespoon dry sherry or balsamic vinegar and 2 to 3 tablespoons chicken stock. Simmer over medium until slightly thickened; season with ¼ teaspoon Chinese five spice.

PEACH JAM

Layer this classic jam with yogurt, fresh fruit, and granola for a tempting breakfast parfait.

① Stir together the peaches and the lemon juice in a 6-quart stainless-steel or enameled Dutch oven. Stir in the pectin. Bring the mixture to a full rolling boil that cannot be stirred down, over high, stirring constantly.

② Add the sugar, stirring to dissolve. Return to a full rolling boil. Boil hard 1 minute, stirring constantly. Remove from heat. Skim the foam, if necessary.

③ Ladle the hot jam into a hot jar, leaving ¼-inch headspace. Wipe the jar rim. Center the lid on the jar. Apply the band, and adjust to fingertip-tight. Place the jar in the boiling water canner. Repeat until all the jars are filled.

④ Process the jars 10 minutes, adjusting for altitude. Turn off heat; remove the lid, and let the jars stand 5 minutes. Remove the jars and cool.

CHANGE IT UP

Peach Cobbler Jam Substitute light brown sugar for the granulated sugar and stir in 1 teaspoon ground cinnamon, ½ teaspoon ground nutmeg, and ¼ teaspoon ground cloves in step 2.

2⅔ cups chopped peeled ripe peaches

2 tablespoons lemon juice

3 tablespoons Ball® Classic Pectin

3⅓ cups sugar

LOW SUGAR

Add ⅔ cup unsweetened fruit juice or water to the peaches and lemon juice, substituting 3 tablespoons Ball® Low or No-Sugar Needed Pectin for the Classic Pectin. Reduce the sugar to 1 cup. This jam will have a looser set than the full-sugar version, but just as much fresh fruit flavor.

PEACH-ROSEMARY JAM

MAKES ABOUT 6 (½-PINT) JARS

**Rosemary lends a delicate flavor twist to the peaches in this jam.
It's equally good on a hot biscuit as it is used as a glaze for grilled shrimp or pork.**

1 Rinse the peaches under cold running water; pat dry. Peel the peaches with a vegetable peeler. Remove the pits, and coarsely chop. Crush with a potato masher until evenly crushed. Measure 4 cups of the crushed peaches into a 6-quart stainless-steel or enameled Dutch oven. Stir in the lime zest and next 3 ingredients.

2 Bring the mixture to a full rolling boil that cannot be stirred down, over high, stirring constantly. Boil 1 minute, stirring constantly.

3 Add the sugar, stirring to dissolve. Return the mixture to a full rolling boil. Boil hard 1 minute, stirring constantly. Remove from heat. Remove and discard rosemary. Skim the foam, if necessary.

4 Ladle the hot jam into a hot jar, leaving ¼-inch headspace. Wipe the jar rim. Center the lid on the jar. Apply the band, and adjust to fingertip-tight. Place the jar in the boiling water canner. Repeat until all the jars are filled.

5 Process the jars 10 minutes, adjusting for altitude. Turn off heat; remove the lid, and let the jars stand 5 minutes. Remove the jars and cool.

2½ pounds fresh peaches (5 large)

1 teaspoon lime zest

6 tablespoons Ball® Classic Pectin

¼ cup fresh lime juice (about 3 limes)

2 (4-inch) rosemary sprigs

5 cups sugar

TIP
Tie the fresh rosemary in a bit of cheesecloth to make removing it easier.

BLUEBERRY JAM

MAKES ABOUT 4 (½-PINT) JARS

**Jump-start your morning with delicious blueberry jam.
Swirl it into yogurt, or warm it and add fresh blueberries to
make a decadent topping for French toast.**

1 pound fresh blueberries

2 tablespoons lemon juice

3 tablespoons Ball® Classic Pectin

3⅓ cups sugar

LOW SUGAR

Add ⅔ cup water or unsweetened fruit juice to the blueberries and lemon juice and substitue 3 tablespoons Ball® Low or No-Sugar Needed Pectin for the Classic Pectin. Reduce the sugar to 1 cup. This jam will have a looser set than the full-sugar version, but just as much delicious fresh fruit flavor.

1 Rinse the berries under cold running water; drain. Crush the berries, 1 layer at a time, with a potato masher until evenly crushed. Measure 2⅔ cups of the crushed blueberries into a 6-quart stainless-steel or enameled Dutch oven.

2 Stir the lemon juice into the crushed blueberries. Stir in the pectin. Bring the mixture to a full rolling boil that cannot be stirred down, over high, stirring constantly.

3 Add the sugar, stirring to dissolve. Return to a full rolling boil. Boil hard 1 minute, stirring constantly. Remove from heat. Skim the foam, if necessary.

4 Ladle the hot jam into a hot jar, leaving ¼-inch headspace. Wipe the jar rim. Center the lid on the jar. Apply the band, and adjust to fingertip-tight. Place the jar in the boiling water canner. Repeat until all the jars are filled.

5 Process the jars 10 minutes, adjusting for altitude. Turn off heat; remove the lid, and let the jars stand 5 minutes. Remove the jars and cool.

BLUEBERRY-LEMON JAM

MAKES ABOUT 4 (½-PINT) JARS

This quick jam is a great way to preserve a bounty of summer blueberries. You can also use frozen blueberries—just measure out the berries before thawing to get the correct volume.

4 cups fresh blueberries

3½ cups sugar

1 teaspoon lemon zest

1 tablespoon lemon juice

1 (3-ounce) pouch Ball® Liquid Pectin

❶ Rinse the blueberries under cold running water; drain. Lightly crush the blueberries with a spoon (just enough to split the skins). Measure 2½ cups of the crushed blueberries into a 6-quart stainless-steel or enameled Dutch oven.

❷ Add the sugar and next 2 ingredients. Bring the mixture to a full rolling boil that cannot be stirred down, over high, stirring constantly.

❸ Add the pectin, immediately squeezing entire contents from the pouch. Continue hard boil for 1 minute, stirring constantly. Remove from heat. Skim the foam, if necessary.

❹ Ladle the hot jam into a hot jar, leaving ¼-inch headspace. Wipe the jar rim. Center the lid on the jar. Apply the band, and adjust to fingertip-tight. Place the jar in the boiling water canner. Repeat until all the jars are filled.

❺ Process the jars 10 minutes, adjusting for altitude. Turn off heat; remove the lid, and let the jars stand 5 minutes. Remove the jars and cool.

TIP
This jam reaches perfection about 3 weeks after canning.

RASPBERRY-HONEY JAM

MAKES ABOUT 6 (½-PINT) JARS

**Using low- or no-sugar needed pectin lets you control the amount
and type of added sweetener in your jam. You can make this jam with
a cup of honey as specified here, or sub in a cup of sugar or an
equivalent amount of a no-calorie sweetener.**

1 Rinse the raspberries under cold running water; drain. Gently crush the raspberries, 1 layer at a time, using a potato masher.

2 Combine the crushed raspberries, water, and pectin in a large stainless-steel or enameled saucepan, stirring to blend the pectin. Bring the mixture to a boil over medium-high, stirring constantly. Add the honey and return the mixture to a boil that cannot be stirred down, over high, stirring constantly. Boil hard for 1 minute, stirring constantly. Remove the mixture from heat if gel begins to form before 1-minute boil is completed. Skim the foam, if necessary.

3 Ladle the hot jam into a hot jar, leaving ¼-inch headspace. Wipe the jar rim. Center the lid on the jar. Apply the band, and adjust to fingertip-tight. Place the jar in the boiling water canner. Repeat until all the jars are filled.

4 Process the jars 10 minutes, adjusting for altitude. Turn off heat; remove the lid, and let the jars stand 5 minutes. Remove the jars and cool.

2½ quarts red raspberries (about 5 to 6 pounds)

1 cup water

5 tablespoons Ball® Low or No-Sugar Needed Pectin

1 cup honey

STRAWBERRY-RHUBARB JAM

MAKES ABOUT 6 (½-PINT) JARS

Bring a burst of flavor and color to croissants or muffins, or try this warmed up as a topping for angel food cake. Combine with fresh strawberries and a dollop of whipped cream to make a quick shortcake.

① Combine the rhubarb and orange juice in a 3-quart stainless-steel or enameled saucepan. Cover and bring to a boil over medium-high. Uncover, reduce heat, and simmer, stirring often, 5 minutes or until the rhubarb is tender.

② Rinse the strawberries under cold running water; drain. Remove the stems and the caps. Crush the strawberries with a potato masher until evenly crushed.

③ Measure 2 cups of the cooked rhubarb and 1¾ cups of the mashed strawberries into a 6-quart stainless-steel or enameled Dutch oven. Stir in the sugar. Bring the mixture to a full rolling boil that cannot be stirred down, over high, stirring frequently.

④ Add the pectin, immediately squeezing entire contents from the pouch. Continue hard boil for 1 minute, stirring constantly. Remove from heat. Skim the foam, if necessary.

⑤ Ladle the hot jam into a hot jar, leaving ¼-inch headspace. Wipe the jar rim. Center the lid on the jar. Apply the band, and adjust to fingertip-tight. Place the jar in the boiling water canner. Repeat until all the jars are filled.

⑥ Process the jars 10 minutes, adjusting for altitude. Turn off heat; remove the lid, and let the jars stand 5 minutes. Remove the jars and cool.

- 4½ cups (¼-inch-thick) sliced fresh rhubarb
- ½ cup fresh orange juice (about 2 to 3 large oranges)
- 4 cups ripe fresh strawberries
- 5 cups sugar
- 1 (3-ounce) pouch Ball® Liquid Pectin

TIP
Choose rhubarb stalks that are ½ to 1 inch in diameter when they are the most tender. If picking your own, make sure to cut off all portions of the leaves because they are poisonous.

MIXED BERRY JAM

Mix and match your favorite berries such as strawberries, blueberries, blackberries, and/or raspberries to create this delightful jam.

2⅔ cups crushed fresh berries (about 1⅓ pounds)

3 tablespoons Ball® Classic Pectin

3⅓ cups sugar

LOW SUGAR

Add ⅔ cup unsweetened fruit juice or water to the berries, substituting 3 tablespoons Ball® Low or No-Sugar Needed Pectin for the Classic Pectin. Reduce the sugar to 1 cup. This jam will have a looser set than the full-sugar version, but just as much fresh fruit flavor.

❶ Place the berries in an 8-quart stainless-steel or enameled Dutch oven. Gradually stir in the pectin. Bring the mixture to a full rolling boil that cannot be stirred down, over high, stirring constantly.

❷ Add the sugar, stirring to dissolve. Return the mixture to a full rolling boil. Boil hard 1 minute, stirring constantly. Remove from heat. Skim the foam, if necessary.

❸ Ladle the hot jam into a hot jar, leaving ¼-inch headspace. Wipe the jar rim. Center the lid on the jar. Apply the band, and adjust to fingertip-tight. Place the jar in the boiling water canner. Repeat until all the jars are filled.

❹ Process the jars 10 minutes, adjusting for altitude. Turn off heat; remove the lid, and let the jars stand 5 minutes. Remove the jars and cool.

. . . . . .

CHANGE IT UP

Instead of a mix of berries, you can chose to use just one. This recipe works well with just raspberries or blackberries.

. . . . . .

BERRY-CHERRY JAM

MAKES ABOUT 6 (½-PINT) JARS

This spread has full-fruit flavor using half the sugar. You can also choose to leave out the sugar altogether. The texture of this jam is thinner than full-sugar versions, but it is just as delicious!

1 quart fresh ripe strawberries (about 2½ to 3 pounds)

2 cups chopped pitted sweet cherries (about 1½ to 2 pounds)

2 cups fresh blackberries (about 1½ to 2 pounds)

1 cup water

3 tablespoons Ball® Low or No-Sugar Needed Pectin

1½ cups sugar (optional)

❶ Rinse the strawberries, cherries, and blackberries under cold running water; drain. Remove the stems and the caps from the strawberries. Crush the strawberries, 1 layer at a time, using a potato masher.

❷ Combine the strawberries, cherries, blackberries, water, and pectin in a large stainless-steel or enameled saucepan, stirring to blend the pectin. Bring the mixture to a boil over high, stirring constantly. Add the sugar, if desired. Return the mixture to a boil that cannot be stirred down. Boil hard for 1 minute, stirring constantly. Remove the mixture from heat if gel begins to form before 1-minute boil is completed. Skim the foam, if necessary.

❸ Ladle the hot jam into a hot jar, leaving ¼-inch headspace. Wipe the jar rim. Center the lid on the jar. Apply the band, and adjust to fingertip-tight. Place the jar in the boiling water canner. Repeat until all the jars are filled.

❹ Process the jars 10 minutes, adjusting for altitude. Turn off heat; remove the lid, and let the jars stand 5 minutes. Remove the jars and cool.

PEAR JAM

MAKES ABOUT 4 (½-PINT) JARS

Ripe pears make a wonderful jam that's yummy on hot buttered biscuits. Choose fragrant pears without soft spots.

1. Stir together the pears and the lemon juice in a 6-quart stainless-steel or enameled Dutch oven. Stir in the pectin. Bring the mixture to a full rolling boil that cannot be stirred down, over high, stirring constantly.

2. Add the sugar, stirring to dissolve. Return to a full rolling boil. Boil hard 1 minute, stirring constantly. Remove from heat. Skim the foam, if necessary.

3. Ladle the hot jam into a hot jar, leaving ¼-inch headspace. Wipe the jar rim. Center the lid on the jar. Apply the band, and adjust to fingertip-tight. Place the jar in the boiling water canner. Repeat until all the jars are filled.

4. Process the jars 10 minutes, adjusting for altitude. Turn off heat; remove the lid, and let the jars stand 5 minutes. Remove the jars and cool.

2⅔ cups finely chopped peeled pears

2 tablespoons lemon juice

3 tablespoons Ball® Classic Pectin

3⅓ cups sugar

LOW SUGAR

Add ⅔ cup unsweetened fruit juice or water to the pears and lemon juice, substituting 3 tablespoons Ball® Low or No-Sugar Needed Pectin for the Classic Pectin. Reduce the sugar to 1 cup. This jam will have a looser set than the full-sugar version, but just as much fresh fruit flavor.

FIG *and* PEAR JAM

MAKES ABOUT 4 (½-PINT) JARS

**Terrific on crostini or as an addition to any cheese board,
this jam can pair as easily with sweet or savory dishes.**

1 Combine the first 5 ingredients in a 6-quart stainless-steel or enameled Dutch oven. Bring the mixture to a full rolling boil that cannot be stirred down, over high, stirring constantly.

2 Add the sugar, stirring to dissolve. Return the mixture to a full rolling boil. Boil hard 1 minute, stirring constantly. Remove from heat. Skim the foam, if necessary.

3 Ladle the hot jam into a hot jar, leaving ¼-inch headspace. Wipe the jar rim. Center the lid on the jar. Apply the band, and adjust to fingertip-tight. Place the jar in the boiling water canner. Repeat until all the jars are filled.

4 Process the jars 10 minutes, adjusting for altitude. Turn off heat; remove the lid, and let the jars stand 5 minutes. Remove the jars and cool.

2 cups chopped peeled pears

2 cups chopped fresh figs

4 tablespoons Ball® Classic Pectin

2 tablespoons bottled lemon juice

1 tablespoon water

3 cups sugar

HONEY-PEAR JAM

MAKES ABOUT 5 (½-PINT) JARS

A bit of apple juice and a little honey offer light sweetness to this delicious gingery pear jam.

3¼ pounds firm, ripe pears, peeled, cored, and chopped

½ cup apple juice

1 tablespoon lemon juice

½ teaspoon ground cinnamon

1 (1-inch) piece fresh ginger, peeled and finely grated*

6 tablespoons Ball® Low or No-Sugar Needed Pectin

½ cup honey

❶ Combine the pears, apple juice, lemon juice, cinnamon, and ginger in a 6-quart stainless-steel or enameled Dutch oven. Cook, uncovered, over medium 15 minutes or until the pears are tender, stirring occasionally. Mash the pear mixture slightly with a potato masher, breaking up large chunks.

❷ Add the pectin, stirring to blend thoroughly. Bring the mixture to a full rolling boil that cannot be stirred down, over high, stirring constantly.

❸ Stir in the honey. Return the mixture to a full rolling boil. Boil hard 1 minute, stirring constantly. Remove from heat. Skim the foam, if necessary.

❹ Ladle the hot jam into a hot jar, leaving ¼-inch headspace. Wipe the jar rim. Center the lid on the jar. Apply the band, and adjust to fingertip-tight. Place the jar in the boiling water canner. Repeat until all the jars are filled.

❺ Process the jars 10 minutes, adjusting for altitude. Turn off heat; remove the lid, and let the jars stand 5 minutes. Remove the jars and cool.

*1 teaspoon ground ginger may be substituted.

CHANGE IT UP

Try mixing pear varieties, such as d'Anjou, Bosc, and Red Bartlett, for different flavor and texture. All are delicious!

PEAR–ROASTED GARLIC PRESERVES

MAKES ABOUT 4 (½-PINT) JARS

**Roasting pears and garlic intensifies their flavor,
creating a sumptuous savory fall treat.**

1 Cut off pointed end of garlic; place garlic on a piece of aluminum foil. Fold foil to seal. Place in corner of a large rimmed baking sheet coated with cooking spray. Arrange the pear wedges in a single layer on the baking sheet. Bake at 400°F for 25 minutes.

2 Turn the pear wedges over; sprinkle with ¼ cup of the sugar. Bake 15 more minutes or until soft. Remove the pan from the oven. Transfer the pear slices to a 6-quart stainless-steel or enameled Dutch oven; add the water. Place the garlic in foil directly on oven rack. Bake 15 more minutes or until soft.

3 Squeeze the pulp from the garlic cloves into the pear mixture. Crush the pear mixture with a potato masher until coarsely chopped. Stir in the vinegar, next 3 ingredients, and remaining 1 cup sugar. Bring to a rolling boil over high. Reduce heat to medium and simmer, uncovered, stirring often to gelling point (220°F).

4 Ladle the hot preserves into a hot jar, leaving ¼-inch headspace. Remove air bubbles. Wipe the jar rim. Center the lid on the jar. Apply the band, and adjust to fingertip-tight. Place the jar in the boiling water canner. Repeat until all the jars are filled.

5 Process the jars 10 minutes, adjusting for altitude. Turn off heat; remove the lid, and let the jars stand 5 minutes. Remove the jars and cool.

1 garlic head

3½ to 4 pounds firm, ripe pears, peeled, cored, and cut into eighths

1¼ cups sugar

½ cup water

¼ cup apple cider vinegar (5% acidity)

1½ teaspoons fresh thyme leaves

½ teaspoon table salt

½ teaspoon freshly ground black pepper

APPLE PIE JAM

MAKES ABOUT 5 (½-PINT) JARS

This jam plays well with graham crackers or ice cream for a sweet pick-me-up.

6 cups diced peeled Granny Smith apples (about 6 apples)

2 cups apple juice or apple cider

2 tablespoons lemon juice

½ cup chopped raisins (optional)

3 tablespoons Ball® Classic Pectin

1 teaspoon ground cinnamon

½ teaspoon ground allspice

¼ teaspoon ground nutmeg

2 cups sugar

1 Bring the apples, juices, and, if desired, raisins to a boil in a 6-quart stainless-steel or enameled Dutch oven; reduce heat, and simmer, uncovered, 10 minutes or until the apples are soft, stirring occasionally.

2 Whisk in the pectin and next 3 ingredients. Bring the mixture to a full rolling boil that cannot be stirred down, over high, stirring constantly.

3 Add the sugar, stirring to dissolve. Return the mixture to a full rolling boil. Boil hard 1 minute, stirring constantly. Remove from heat. Skim the foam, if necessary.

4 Ladle the hot jam into a hot jar, leaving ¼-inch headspace. Wipe the jar rim. Center the lid on the jar. Apply the band, and adjust to fingertip-tight. Place the jar in the boiling water canner. Repeat until all the jars are filled.

5 Process the jars 10 minutes, adjusting for altitude. Turn off heat; remove the lid, and let the jars stand 5 minutes. Remove the jars and cool.

APPLE PRESERVES

What could be more delightful than tender slices of fruit suspended in a delicately flavored syrup?

6 or 7 large apples, peeled, cored, and cut into ¼- to ⅓-inch slices

1 large lemon

1 cup water

6 tablespoons Ball® Classic Pectin

4 cups sugar

2 teaspoons ground nutmeg

❶ Rinse the apples and lemon under cold running water; pat dry. Peel, core, and slice the apples. Measure 6 cups of the sliced apples. Cut the lemon in half and remove the seeds. Extract the juice from half of the lemon. Thinly slice remaining half of the lemon, discarding end.

❷ Combine the apples, water, and lemon juice in a large stainless-steel or enameled saucepan. Cover; simmer the apples 10 minutes over medium. Add the pectin, stirring to blend thoroughly. Bring the mixture to a boil over medium-high, stirring constantly. Add the lemon slices, sugar, and nutmeg, stirring until the sugar dissolves. Bring the mixture to a rolling boil that cannot be stirred down. Boil hard for 1 minute, stirring constantly. Remove from heat. Skim the foam, if necessary.

❸ Ladle the hot preserves into a hot jar, leaving ¼-inch headspace. Remove air bubbles. Wipe the jar rim. Center the lid on the jar. Apply the band, and adjust to fingertip-tight. Place the jar in the boiling water canner. Repeat until all the jars are filled.

❹ Process the jars 10 minutes, adjusting for altitude. Turn off heat; remove the lid, and let the jars stand 5 minutes. Remove the jars and cool.

CHANGE IT UP

You can substitute ground cinnamon or pumpkin pie spice for the nutmeg. Adjust the measurement as desired.

CHERRY-RASPBERRY PRESERVES

MAKES 4 TO 6 (½-PINT) JARS

Summery raspberries and cherries marry in this perfect blend of sweet and tart.

① Rinse the cherries under cold running water; drain. Stem and pit the cherries. Coarsely chop the cherries. If desired, press the raspberries through a mesh strainer to remove seeds before measuring.

② Combine the cherries, raspberries, fruit juice, and lemon juice in an 8-quart stainless-steel or enameled Dutch oven. Whisk in the pectin until dissolved. Bring the fruit mixture to a boil over high, stirring constantly. If using, add the sugar and return the mixture to a boil. Stirring frequently, boil 3 minutes. Remove from heat. Skim the foam, if necessary.

③ Ladle the preserves into a hot jar, leaving ¼-inch-headspace. Remove air bubbles. Wipe the jar rim. Center the lid on the jar. Apply the band, and adjust to fingertip-tight. Place the jar in the boiling water canner. Repeat until all the jars are filled.

④ Process the jars 10 minutes, adjusting for altitude. Turn off heat; remove the lid, and let the jars stand 5 minutes. Remove the jars and cool.

3 cups coarsley chopped pitted sweet cherries (about 1½ pounds)

1 cup crushed fresh raspberries

1 cup unsweetened raspberry, cranberry, or apple juice

2 tablespoons lemon juice

6 tablespoons Ball® Low or No-Sugar Needed Pectin

1½ cups sugar (optional)

TIP

If using sugar, adjust the quantity to desired sweetness, staying within a 1- to 3-cup range. Keep in mind that the less sugar used, the looser your set will be.

TRADITIONAL CHERRY PRESERVES

MAKES ABOUT 4 (½-PINT) JARS

Long cooking without added pectin is the traditional way to make jams and preserves. The extra cook time allows for a more concentrated flavor, but yields less jam volume.

1 Rinse the cherries under cold running water; drain. Remove the stems and pits from cherries over a bowl to retain all juices. Set aside the pitted cherries.

2 Combine the cherry juice and the sugar in a large stainless-steel or enameled saucepan. Bring the mixture to a boil, stirring until the sugar dissolves. Add a small amount of water if there is not enough juice to dissolve the sugar. Add the cherries. Boil over high until the cherries become glossy. Remove from heat. Cover and let stand in the refrigerator 12 to 18 hours. Bring the mixture to a rolling boil that cannot be stirred down. Cook rapidly over high almost to gelling point (220°F) (page 18), stirring constantly. Remove from heat. Skim the foam, if necessary.

3 Ladle the hot preserves into a hot jar, leaving ¼-inch headspace. Remove air bubbles. Wipe the jar rim. Center the lid on the jar. Apply the band, and adjust to fingertip-tight. Place the jar in the boiling water canner. Repeat until all the jars are filled.

4 Process the jars 10 minutes, adjusting for altitude. Turn off heat; remove the lid, and let the jars stand 5 minutes. Remove the jars and cool.

2 pounds cherries

4 cups sugar

CHANGE IT UP

Berry Preserves Substitute 2 pounds of any combination of berries, including blackberries, red or black raspberries, or loganberries for the cherries in this recipe. Rinse the berries under cold running water; drain. Combine the berries with the sugar in a large stainless-steel or enameled saucepan and let the mixture stand until the juices begin to flow, about 10 minutes. Bring to a boil, stirring until the sugar dissolves. Cook rapidly over high almost to the gelling point (220°F), stirring constantly. Remove from heat. Skim the foam, if necessary. Follow steps 3 and 4.

JAMS, PRESERVES, and MARMALADES

CHOCOLATE-RASPBERRY SAUCE

MAKES ABOUT 6 (½-PINT) JARS

Though this chocolate-raspberry sauce is technically not a jam, the method is very similar so it is included here. This sauce is decadent, rich, and fantastically versatile. Serve it over ice cream, cheesecake, or fruit. It makes a sure-to-be-appreciated hostess gift.

½ cup sifted unsweetened cocoa powder

6 tablespoons Ball® Classic Pectin

4½ cups crushed red raspberries

4 tablespoons lemon juice

6¾ cups sugar

❶ Combine the cocoa powder and pectin in a medium glass bowl, stirring until evenly blended.

❷ Combine the crushed raspberries and lemon juice in a large stainless-steel or enameled saucepan. Whisk in the pectin mixture until dissolved. Bring to a boil over high, stirring frequently. Add the sugar and return to a full rolling boil, stirring constantly. Boil hard for 1 minute, stirring constantly. Remove from heat. Skim the foam, if necessary.

❸ Ladle the hot sauce into a hot jar, leaving ¼-inch headspace. Remove air bubbles. Wipe the jar rim. Center the lid on the jar. Apply the band, and adjust to fingertip-tight. Place the jar in the boiling water canner. Repeat until all the jars are filled.

❹ Process the jars for 10 minutes, adjusting for altitude. Turn off heat; remove the lid, and let the jars stand 5 minutes. Remove the jars and cool.

KIWI PRESERVES

The beautiful color and unique flavor of these preserves make them another excellent choice for gift giving.

① Peel the kiwifruit and slice crosswise into ⅛-inch slices.

② Combine the kiwifruit, sugar, pineapple juice, and lime juice in a large stainless-steel or enameled saucepan. Bring the mixture to a boil, stirring until the sugar dissolves. Add the pectin, immediately squeezing entire contents from the pouch. Bring the mixture to a rolling boil that cannot be stirred down. Boil hard for 1 minute, stirring constantly. Remove from heat. Skim the foam, if necessary.

③ Ladle the hot preserves into a hot jar, leaving ¼-inch headspace. Remove air bubbles. Wipe the jar rim. Center the lid on the jar. Apply the band, and adjust to fingertip-tight. Place the jar in the boiling water canner. Repeat until all the jars are filled.

④ Process the jars 10 minutes, adjusting for altitude. Turn off heat; remove the lid, and let the jars stand 5 minutes. Remove the jars and cool.

4 large kiwifruit

3 cups sugar

¾ cup unsweetened pineapple juice

¼ cup fresh lime juice

1 (3-ounce) pouch Ball® Liquid Pectin

PAPAYA-GRAPEFRUIT PRESERVES

MAKES ABOUT 7 (½-PINT) JARS

**Home-canning doesn't have to be limited to summer and fall.
These winter/spring fruits make delicious soft spreads.**

2 large grapefruit

2 cups chopped peeled papaya
or mango

¼ cup water

6 tablespoons Ball® Classic Pectin

3½ cups sugar

2 tablespoons orange liqueur
(optional)

❶ Scrub the grapefruit thoroughly; rinse well, and pat dry. Grate the grapefruit peel to equal 2 tablespoons. With a sharp knife, remove remaining peel and pith from the grapefruit; discard. Working over a bowl to catch the juice, remove the grapefruit segments; discard membrane. Measure 2 cups of the grapefruit, including juice.

❷ Combine the grapefruit peel, segments, and juice with the papaya and water in a 6-quart stainless-steel or enameled Dutch oven. Stir in the pectin. Bring the mixture to a boil over high, stirring constantly.

❸ Add the sugar and return the mixture to a boil that cannot be stirred down. Boil hard for 1 minute, stirring constantly. Remove from heat. Skim the foam, if necessary. Stir in the orange liqueur, if desired.

❹ Ladle the hot preserves into a hot jar, leaving ½-inch headspace. Remove air bubbles. Wipe the jar rim. Center the lid on the jar. Apply the band, and adjust to fingertip-tight. Place the jar in the boiling water canner. Repeat until all the jars are filled.

❺ Process the jars 10 minutes, adjusting for altitude. Turn off heat; remove the lid, and let the jars stand 5 minutes. Remove the jars and cool.

EASIEST EVER MARMALADE

MAKES ABOUT 6 (½-PINT) JARS

A food processor speeds up fruit preparation in this uniquely flavored marmalade. Maraschino cherries add a touch of brightness to the light amber color.

3 small oranges, unpeeled

1 lemon, unpeeled

1 small grapefruit, unpeeled

2 cups canned crushed pineapple, undrained

6 cups sugar

½ teaspoon butter (optional)

½ cup chopped maraschino cherries

❶ Rinse the oranges, lemon, and grapefruit under cold running water; pat dry. Coarsely chop the oranges, lemon, and grapefruit; remove and discard the seeds. Process the fruit in a food processor until finely chopped.

❷ Combine the prepared fruit, pineapple, and sugar in a large stainless-steel or enameled saucepan. Bring to a boil, stirring until the sugar dissolves. If desired, add ½ teaspoon butter to reduce foaming. Stirring frequently to prevent scorching, boil gently, uncovered, 25 minutes or until the marmalade reaches gelling point (220°F). Stir in the cherries during the last 5 minutes.

❸ Ladle the hot marmalade into a hot jar, leaving ¼-inch headspace. Remove air bubbles. Wipe the jar rim. Center the lid on the jar. Apply the band, and adjust to fingertip-tight. Place the jar in the boiling water canner. Repeat until all the jars are filled.

❹ Process the jars 10 minutes, adjusting for altitude. Turn off heat; remove the lid, and let the jars stand 5 minutes. Remove the jars and cool.

BLOOD ORANGE–GINGER MARMALADE

MAKES ABOUT 6 (½-PINT) JARS

This recipe takes 2 days to prepare. Boiling and soaking aids in the breakdown of tough citrus membranes and softens the rind so that sectioning isn't necessary.

1 Rinse the oranges under cold running water; pat dry. Quarter 6 of the oranges lengthwise. Cut the quarters crosswise into thin slices. Place the orange slices in a large stainless-steel or enameled saucepan; add water to cover. Bring to a boil. Remove from heat; cover and let stand at room temperature 8 hours or overnight.

2 Next day, squeeze the juice from the remaining 6 blood oranges into a 1-quart glass measuring cup; discard rinds or reserve for another use.

3 Use a slotted spoon to transfer the blood orange slices to a 6-quart stainless-steel or enameled Dutch oven, reserving the soaking liquid. Add enough of the soaking liquid to the blood orange juice to measure 4 cups. Discard remaining soaking liquid.

4 Add the blood orange juice mixture, sugar, and next 2 ingredients to the orange slices. Bring to a rolling boil over high; reduce heat to medium and simmer, uncovered, stirring often to gelling point (220°F).

5 Ladle the hot marmalade into a hot jar, leaving ¼-inch headspace. Remove air bubbles. Wipe the jar rim. Center the lid on the jar. Apply the band, and adjust to fingertip-tight. Place the jar in the boiling water canner. Repeat until all the jars are filled.

6 Process the jars 10 minutes, adjusting for altitude. Turn off heat; remove the lid, and let the jars stand 5 minutes. Remove the jars and cool.

4½ to 5 pounds blood oranges, unpeeled (about 12)

8 cups sugar

¼ cup lemon juice (about 2 lemons)

2 teaspoons grated peeled fresh ginger

RHUBARB-ORANGE MARMALADE

MAKES ABOUT 8 (½-PINT) JARS

Think outside the jar: This marmalade is delicious on roasted meats or a toasted bagel smeared with cream cheese.

❶ Rinse the oranges under cold running water; pat dry. Cut each orange half into quarters. Process the orange pieces in a food processor until coarsely chopped.

❷ Combine the chopped orange, rhubarb, and sugar in a 6-quart stainless-steel or enameled Dutch oven. Bring to a boil; reduce heat, and simmer 1 hour or until gelling point (220°F).

❸ Ladle the hot marmalade into a hot jar, leaving ¼-inch headspace. Remove air bubbles. Wipe the jar rim. Center the lid on the jar. Apply the band, and adjust to fingertip-tight. Place the jar in the boiling water canner. Repeat until all the jars are filled.

❹ Process the jars 10 minutes, adjusting for altitude. Turn off heat; remove the lid, and let the jars stand 5 minutes. Remove the jars and cool.

2 oranges, unpeeled, halved crosswise and seeded

6 cups (1-inch slices) fresh or frozen rhubarb

6 cups sugar

TIP

Beginning with orange pieces that are the same size will ensure that they are more evenly chopped in the food processor.

ORANGE-CHILE MARMALADE

MAKES ABOUT 8 (½-PINT) JARS

**Chile peppers intensify the citrus flavor and add zing to
this unique marmalade. Use it to enhance cheese trays,
or serve it as a condiment with battered shrimp.**

2¼ pounds oranges, unpeeled, seeded, and thinly sliced

Zest and juice of 1 lemon

6 cups water

3 dried habanero chile peppers (or 6 dried Colorado or New Mexico chile peppers)

9 cups sugar

½ teaspoon butter (optional)

❶ Combine the oranges, lemon zest, juice, and water in a stainless-steel or enameled Dutch oven. Bring to a boil over high, stirring constantly. Reduce heat and boil gently, stirring occasionally, for 40 minutes. Add the chile peppers, partially cover, and boil gently, stirring occasionally, until the fruit is very soft, about 30 minutes. Remove and discard the chile peppers.

❷ Bring the mixture to a boil over medium-high, stirring constantly. Maintaining a boil, gradually stir in the sugar. If desired, add ½ teaspoon butter to reduce foaming. Boil hard, stirring occasionally, about 15 minutes or until the mixture reaches gelling point (220°F). Remove from heat and test gel. If gel stage has been reached, skim the foam.

❸ Ladle the hot marmalade into a hot jar, leaving ¼-inch headspace. Remove air bubbles. Wipe the jar rim. Center the lid on the jar. Apply the band, and adjust to fingertip-tight. Place the jar in the boiling water canner. Repeat until all the jars are filled.

❹ Process the jars 10 minutes, adjusting for altitude. Turn off heat; remove the lid, and let the jars stand 5 minutes. Remove the jars and cool.

RED ONION–CRANBERRY MARMALADE

MAKES ABOUT 5 (½-PINT) JARS

Serve this with pork tenderloin or duck.

1 Rinse the orange under cold running water; pat dry. Grate the orange zest to equal 2 teaspoons.

2 Sauté the onions, dried cranberries, brown sugar, and vinegar in a skillet until the onions are transparent. Combine the onion mixture, pectin, orange zest, and apple juice in a large stainless-steel or enameled saucepan. Bring the mixture to a boil over medium-high, stirring constantly. Add the granulated sugar, stirring until the sugar dissolves. Return the mixture to a rolling boil that cannot be stirred down. Boil hard 1 minute, stirring constantly. Remove from heat. Skim foam, if necessary.

3 Ladle the hot marmalade into a hot jar, leaving ¼-inch headspace. Remove air bubbles. Wipe the jar rim. Center the lid on the jar. Apply the band, and adjust to fingertip-tight. Place the jar in the boiling water canner. Repeat until all the jars are filled.

4 Process the jars 15 minutes, adjusting for altitude. Turn off heat; remove the lid, and let the jars stand 5 minutes. Remove the jars and cool.

1 small orange

1½ cups thinly sliced red onions (about 1 to 1½ pounds)

½ cup finely chopped dried cranberries (about ½ pound)

¼ cup packed light brown sugar

¼ cup apple cider vinegar (5% acidity)

6 tablespoons Ball® Classic Pectin

3 cups bottled unsweetened apple juice

4 cups granulated sugar

MEYER LEMON MARMALADE

MAKES ABOUT 5 (½-PINT) JARS

Meyer lemons have a brief season and are worth finding just to make this marmalade. This recipe is a two-day process as it requires an overnight resting of fruit and juice.

2 pounds Meyer lemons, unpeeled

2 regular lemons, unpeeled

6 cups water

5 cups sugar

¼ cup lemon juice (about 2 lemons)

1 Rinse the lemons under cold running water; pat dry. Cut 1 pound of the Meyer lemons and the regular lemons lengthwise into quarters, and place in a 6-quart stainless-steel or enameled Dutch oven. Add 3 cups of the water. Bring to a boil; reduce heat, and simmer, uncovered, 1 hour and 30 minutes or until the lemons are very soft and the liquid is syrupy, pressing the lemons to release juice. Remove from heat, cover, and let stand at room temperature overnight.

2 While the quartered lemons are simmering, quarter the remaining Meyer lemons lengthwise; remove the seeds, and cut crosswise into very thin slices. Place in a 6-quart stainless-steel or enameled Dutch oven. Add the remaining water (just enough to cover the lemon slices). Bring to a boil; reduce heat, and simmer, uncovered, 30 minutes, stirring occasionally. Remove from heat; cover and let stand at room temperature overnight.

3 Pour the lemon quarters mixture through a mesh strainer into the Dutch oven containing the lemon slices, pressing with the back of a wooden spoon to extract as much juice as possible. Discard the solids. Add the sugar and the lemon juice to the lemon slices. Bring to a rolling boil over high; reduce heat to medium, and cook, uncovered, stirring often, 45 minutes or to gelling point (220°F).

4 Ladle the hot marmalade into a hot jar, leaving ¼-inch headspace. Remove air bubbles. Wipe the jar rim. Center the lid on the jar. Apply the band, and adjust to fingertip-tight. Place the jar in the boiling water canner. Repeat until all the jars are filled.

5 Process the jars 10 minutes, adjusting for altitude. Turn off heat; remove the lid, and let the jars stand 5 minutes. Remove the jars and cool.

QUICK-SET GRAPEFRUIT MARMALADE

This sunny pink marmalade has more perk and less bite than its traditional English cousin.

❶ Scrub the fruit thoroughly under cold running water; rinse, and pat dry. Carefully strip the zest from the grapefruit and the lemon with a vegetable peeler, avoiding the bitter white pith. Coarsely chop the zest to measure 1 cup. Place the zest, water, and baking soda in a 6-quart stainless-steel or enameled Dutch oven. Bring to a boil over high; cover, reduce heat, and simmer, stirring occasionally, 20 minutes.

❷ Using a sharp, thin-bladed knife, cut a ¼-inch-thick slice from each end of the grapefruits and the lemon. Place flat-end down on a cutting board, and remove and discard peel (bitter white pith and any remaining rind) in strips, cutting from top to bottom, and following the curvature of the fruit. Holding the peeled fruit in the palm of your hand and working over a bowl to collect the juices, slice between the membranes, and gently remove whole segments. Discard the membranes and seeds. Coarsely chop the fruit to measure 2¼ cups fruit and juices.

❸ Add the fruit and the juices to the zest in the pan. Bring to a boil; reduce heat, and simmer, uncovered, stirring often, 10 minutes.

❹ Stir in the pectin. Bring the mixture to a full rolling boil that cannot be stirred down, over high, stirring constantly.

❺ Add the sugar, stirring to dissolve. Return the mixture to a full rolling boil. Boil hard 1 minute, stirring constantly. Remove from heat. Skim the foam, if necessary.

❻ Ladle the hot marmalade into a hot jar, leaving ¼-inch headspace. Remove air bubbles. Wipe the jar rim. Center the lid on the jar. Apply the band, and adjust to fingertip-tight. Place the jar in the boiling water canner. Repeat until all the jars are filled.

❼ Process the jars 10 minutes, adjusting for altitude. Turn off heat; remove lid, and let the jars stand 5 minutes. Remove the jars and cool.

3 large red grapefruit, unpeeled (about 2¾ pounds)

1 lemon, unpeeled

2½ cups water

⅛ teaspoon baking soda

6 tablespoons Ball® Classic Pectin

4 cups sugar

2

JELLIES

Homemade jellies feature juice extracted from
fresh fruits and vegetables, or bottled juices. The
strained juice makes these spreads translucent
and shimmery while the pectin produces
a firm texture.

HOW TO MAKE JELLIES

You will need:

- Tested recipe and ingredients
- Glass preserving jars with lids and bands (always start with new lids)
- Water bath canner or a large, deep stockpot with lid and rack
- Jar lifter
- Common kitchen utensils, including measuring cups and spoons, large ladle, kitchen towel, and rubber spatula
- Large stainless-steel or enameled saucepan or Dutch oven
- Mesh strainer
- Cheesecloth
- Canning funnel
- Bubble remover and headspace measuring tool
- Labels

TIPS

You may also use a dishwasher to wash and heat the jars.

Rinse fruit under cold running water instead of soaking.

To avoid cloudy jelly, do not press or squeeze the fruit mixture while the juice strains.

If the juice cannot be used immediately, it may be canned or frozen to use later.

STEP 1: HEAT JARS Examine the jars for defects. Place a canning rack at the bottom of the canner and fill halfway with water. Place the jars in the water and bring almost to a simmer over medium. **IMPORTANT:** Keep the jars hot until ready to fill to prevent jar breakage due to thermal shock. Wash lids and bands in warm soapy water, rinse, and set aside.

STEP 2: EXTRACT JUICE Prepare the ingredients according to the recipe. Crush the fruit if noted in the recipe. Bring the fruit, plus water and lemon juice, if noted, to a boil in a stainless-steel or enameled Dutch oven. Cover, reduce heat, and simmer 10 minutes.

Drain the mixture through a strainer lined with 3 layers of dampened cheesecloth. Drain 2 to 4 hours or until correct amount of juice is extracted. Transfer it to a container and refrigerate overnight. When ready to use, ladle the juice from the top to avoid disturbing any pulp that may have settled at the bottom.

STEP 3: COOK Combine the juice and pectin in a large stainless-steel saucepan. Stirring constantly, bring the mixture to a rolling boil that cannot be stirred down. Stir in the sugar. Return to a full rolling boil. Boil hard 1 minute, stirring constantly. Remove from heat. Skim off foam, if necessary.

STEP 4: FILL Using a ladle and canning funnel, fill a hot jar with the hot jelly, leaving ¼-inch headspace. Wipe the rim and top of the jar with a clean, damp cloth to remove any food residue, which can prevent a vacuum seal.

STEP 5: Center the lid on the jar, allowing sealing compound to come in contact with the jar rim. Apply the band and adjust until fit is fingertip-tight. Make sure the band is not overtightened—air inside the jars must be able to escape during canning.

STEP 6: Place the filled jar in the canner. Repeat one at a time until all the jars are filled. (If using a canning rack, lower the rack with the jars the into water.) Make sure the water covers the jars by at least 1 inch. Add more hot water if needed.

STEP 7: PROCESS Place the lid on the canner and bring the water to a full rolling boil. Once the water is fully boiling, start timing for the length of time stated in the recipe (adjusting for altitude, page 16). Maintain a rolling boil throughout the entire processing period. Turn off the heat and remove the lid. Let the canner cool 5 minutes before removing the jars.

STEP 8: Using the jar lifter, remove the jars from the canner and set upright on a towel or cutting board, leaving at least 2 inches between the jars. Leave the jars undisturbed for at least 12 hours. Bands may loosen during processing but should not be retightened, as this may interfere with the sealing process.

STEP 9: TEST & STORE Check the lids for vacuum seals after stand time. Lids should not flex up and down when the center is pressed. Remove the bands. Gently try to lift off the lids with your fingertips. If the lid cannot be lifted off, the lid has a good seal. Wipe the jars and lids with a clean, damp cloth. Label and store in a cool, dry, dark place up to 1 year.

STRAWBERRY JELLY

MAKES ABOUT 4 (½-PINT) JARS

Make this classic jelly in the spring when strawberries are at their peak.

8 pounds firm, ripe strawberries, hulled

Cheesecloth

4 tablespoons Ball® Classic Pectin

3⅓ cups sugar

LOW SUGAR

Increase the strawberries to 13 pounds to collect 4⅔ cups strawberry juice. Substitute 4 tablespoons Ball® Low or No-Sugar Needed Pectin for the Classic Pectin and reduce the sugar to 1 cup. This jelly will have a looser set than the full-sugar version, but even more fresh fruit flavor.

❶ Rinse the strawberries under cold running water; drain. Crush the strawberries, 1 layer at a time, with a potato masher, in a 6-quart stainless-steel or enameled Dutch oven. Bring to a boil. Cover; reduce heat, and simmer 5 minutes.

❷ Pour the strawberries through a mesh strainer lined with 3 layers of dampened cheesecloth into a bowl. Let drain 2 to 4 hours or until the juice measures 3 cups. (To avoid cloudy jelly, do not press or squeeze the strawberries.)

❸ Combine the strawberry juice and the pectin in a 6-quart stainless-steel or enameled Dutch oven. Bring the mixture to a rolling boil that cannot be stirred down, over high, stirring constantly.

❹ Add the sugar, stirring to dissolve. Return to a full rolling boil. Boil hard 1 minute, stirring constantly. Remove from heat. Skim the foam, if necessary.

❺ Ladle the hot jelly into a hot jar, leaving ¼-inch headspace. Wipe the jar rim. Center the lid on the jar. Apply the band, and adjust to fingertip-tight. Place the jar in the boiling water canner. Repeat until all the jars are filled.

❻ Process the jars 10 minutes, adjusting for altitude. Turn off heat; remove the lid, and let the jars stand 5 minutes. Remove the jars and cool.

CHANGE IT UP

Strawberry-Balsamic Jelly Follow the recipe, adding 1 to 2 tablespoons good-quality balsamic vinegar to the juice mixture in step 3.

BERRY JELLY

**This vibrant jelly is a wonderful way to use a wealth of
wild berries. Delicate berries can get moldy quickly so don't
rinse them until you're ready to begin.**

❶ Rinse the berries under cold running water; drain. Crush the
berries, 1 layer at a time, with a potato masher in a 6-quart stainless-
steel or enameled Dutch oven. Cover and bring to a boil; reduce
heat, and simmer 5 minutes.

❷ Pour the berry mixture through a mesh strainer lined with 3
layers of dampened cheesecloth into a bowl. Let drain 2 to 4 hours
or until the juice measures 3 cups. (To avoid cloudy jelly, do not
press or squeeze the berry mixture.)

❸ Combine the berry juice and the pectin in a 6-quart stainless-steel
or enameled Dutch oven. Bring the mixture to a rolling boil that
cannot be stirred down, over high, stirring constantly.

❹ Add the sugar, stirring to dissolve. Return to a full rolling boil.
Boil hard 1 minute, stirring constantly. Remove from heat. Skim
the foam, if necessary.

❺ Ladle the hot jelly into a hot jar, leaving ¼-inch headspace.
Wipe the jar rim. Center the lid on the jar. Apply the band, and
adjust to fingertip-tight. Place the jar in the boiling water canner.
Repeat until all the jars are filled.

❻ Process the jars 10 minutes, adjusting for altitude. Turn off heat;
remove the lid, and let the jars stand 5 minutes. Remove the jars
and cool.

3 pounds blackberries or
   raspberries

Cheesecloth

4 tablespoons Ball® Classic Pectin

3⅓ cups sugar

LOW SUGAR

Increase the berries to 4 pounds
to collect 4⅔ cups berry juice.
Substitute 4 tablespoons Ball®
Low or No-Sugar Needed Pectin
for the Classic Pectin and reduce
the sugar to 1 cup. This jelly
will have a looser set than the
full-sugar version, but even more
fresh fruit flavor.

CHANGE IT UP

Berry-Pepper Jelly To add a nutty, savory background flavor, toast
1 teaspoon of freshly cracked black pepper for 30 seconds in a
very hot skillet. Add to the juice mixture in step 3.

JELLIES

RED PLUM–RASPBERRY JELLY

Plums economically extend more expensive raspberries in this pretty red jelly. Perfect for spreading on scones or biscuits, it can also be used to fill linzer or thumbprint cookies.

2 pounds firm, ripe red plums, halved

1 cup water

4 cups raspberries (about 5 [6-ounce] containers)

Cheesecloth

4 tablespoons Ball® Classic Pectin

3⅓ cups sugar

1. Pit and chop the plums, and place in a 6-quart stainless-steel or enameled Dutch oven. Lightly crush the plums with a potato masher. Stir in the water. Bring to a boil; reduce heat, cover, and simmer 10 minutes. Add the raspberries, crushing with the potato masher. Return to a boil; cover, reduce heat, and simmer 10 minutes.

2. Pour the plum mixture through a mesh strainer lined with 3 layers of dampened cheesecloth into a bowl. Let drain 3 hours or until the juice measures 3½ cups. Wash and dry the Dutch oven.

3. Stir together the juice and the pectin in same Dutch oven. Bring the mixture to a full rolling boil that cannot be stirred down, over high, stirring constantly.

4. Add the sugar, stirring to dissolve. Return the mixture to a full rolling boil. Boil hard 1 minute, stirring constantly. Remove from heat. Skim the foam, if necessary.

5. Ladle the hot jelly into a hot jar, leaving ¼-inch headspace. Wipe the jar rim. Center the lid on the jar. Apply the band, and adjust to fingertip-tight. Place the jar in the boiling water canner. Repeat until all the jars are filled.

6. Process the jars 10 minutes, adjusting for altitude. Turn off heat; remove the lid, and let the jars stand 5 minutes. Remove the jars and cool.

TIP

Plum pits are high in pectin, so simmering them with the fruit helps give this jelly its velvety smooth set.

CURRANT JELLY

This sweet-tart jelly is delicious paired with savory lamb, venison, and pork.

3⅓ pounds red currants or
   black currants

¼ cup water

Cheesecloth

4 tablespoons Ball® Classic Pectin

3⅓ cups sugar

LOW SUGAR

Increase the currants to 4½ pounds to collect 4⅔ cups currant juice. Substitute 4 tablespoons Ball® Low or No-Sugar Needed Pectin for the Classic Pectin and reduce the sugar to 1 cup. This jelly will have a looser set than the full-sugar version, but even more fresh fruit flavor.

❶ Rinse the currants under running water; drain. Crush the currants, 1 layer at a time, with a potato masher in a 6-quart stainless-steel or enameled Dutch oven. Stir in the water. Bring to a boil; reduce heat, and simmer 10 minutes.

❷ Pour the currant mixture through a mesh strainer lined with 3 layers of dampened cheesecloth into a bowl. Let drain 2 to 4 hours or until the juice measures 3 cups. (To avoid cloudy jelly, do not press or squeeze the currant mixture.)

❸ Combine the currant juice and the pectin in a 6-quart stainless-steel or enameled Dutch oven. Bring the mixture to a rolling boil that cannot be stirred down, over high, stirring constantly.

❹ Add the sugar, stirring to dissolve. Return to a full rolling boil. Boil hard 1 minute, stirring constantly. Remove from heat. Skim the foam, if necessary.

❺ Ladle the hot jelly into a hot jar, leaving ¼-inch headspace. Wipe the jar rim. Center the lid on the jar. Apply the band, and adjust to fingertip-tight. Place the jar in the boiling water canner. Repeat until all the jars are filled.

❻ Process the jars 10 minutes, adjusting for altitude. Turn off heat; remove the lid, and let the jars stand 5 minutes. Remove the jars and cool.

SWEET CHERRY JELLY

MAKES ABOUT 4 (½-PINT) JARS

Bing cherries are the most common sweet cherries. Look for firm, glossy fruit with stems still attached. The deeper the color, the richer the flavor.

❶ Bring the cherries, water, and the lemon juice to a boil in a 6-quart stainless-steel or enameled Dutch oven. Cover; reduce heat, and simmer 10 minutes.

❷ Pour the cherry mixture through a mesh strainer lined with 3 layers of dampened cheesecloth into a bowl. Let drain 2 to 4 hours or until the juice measures 3 cups. (To avoid cloudy jelly, do not press or squeeze the cherry mixture.)

❸ Combine the cherry juice and the pectin in a 6-quart stainless-steel or enameled Dutch oven. Bring the mixture to a rolling boil that cannot be stirred down, over high, stirring constantly.

❹ Add the sugar, stirring to dissolve. Return to a full rolling boil. Boil hard 1 minute, stirring constantly. Remove from heat. Skim the foam, if necessary.

❺ Ladle the hot jelly into a hot jar, leaving ¼-inch headspace. Wipe the jar rim. Center the lid on the jar. Apply the band, and adjust to fingertip-tight. Place the jar in the boiling water canner. Repeat until all the jars are filled.

❻ Process the jars 10 minutes, adjusting for altitude. Turn off heat; remove the lid, and let the jars stand 5 minutes. Remove the jars and cool.

3 pounds dark sweet cherries, stemmed, pitted, and finely chopped

⅓ cup water

2 tablespoons lemon juice

Cheesecloth

4 tablespoons Ball® Classic Pectin

3⅓ cups sugar

LOW SUGAR

Increase the cherries to 4 pounds and water to ½ cup to collect 4⅔ cups cherry juice. Substitute 4 tablespoons Ball® Low or No-Sugar Needed Pectin for the Classic Pectin and reduce the sugar to 1 cup. This jelly will have a looser set than the full-sugar version, but even more fresh fruit flavor.

CHANGE IT UP

Add a pinch or two of dried chipotle chile pepper to add some smoky heat to the sweet cherry flavor.

SOUR CHERRY JELLY

MAKES ABOUT 6 (½-PINT) JARS

Try this with ham on hot rolls, or stir a few spoonfuls of Sour Cherry Jelly into your lemonade to create Sour Cherry Lemonade.

3 pounds tart red cherries, stemmed, pitted, and chopped

⅓ cup water

Cheesecloth

4 tablespoons Ball® Classic Pectin

3⅓ cups sugar

LOW SUGAR

Increase the cherries to 4 pounds and water to ½ cup to collect 4⅔ cups cherry juice. Substitute 4 tablespoons Ball® Low or No-Sugar Needed Pectin for the Classic Pectin and reduce the sugar to 1 cup. This jelly will have a looser set than the full-sugar version, but even more fresh fruit flavor.

1 Bring the cherries and water to a boil in a 6-quart stainless-steel or enameled Dutch oven. Cover; reduce heat, and simmer 10 minutes.

2 Pour the cherry mixture through a mesh strainer lined with 3 layers of dampened cheesecloth into a bowl. Let drain 2 to 4 hours or until the juice measures 3 cups. (To avoid cloudy jelly, do not press or squeeze the cherry mixture.)

3 Combine the cherry juice and the pectin in a 6-quart stainless-steel or enameled Dutch oven. Bring the mixture to a rolling boil that cannot be stirred down, over high, stirring constantly.

4 Add the sugar, stirring to dissolve. Return to a full rolling boil. Boil hard 1 minute, stirring constantly. Remove from heat. Skim the foam, if necessary.

5 Ladle the hot jelly into a hot jar, leaving ¼-inch headspace. Wipe the jar rim. Center the lid on the jar. Apply the band, and adjust to fingertip-tight. Place the jar in the boiling water canner. Repeat until all the jars are filled.

6 Process the jars 10 minutes, adjusting for altitude. Turn off heat; remove the lid, and let the jars stand 5 minutes. Remove the jars and cool.

PLUM JELLY

MAKES ABOUT 4 (½-PINT) JARS

**Savor the juicy sweet goodness of late-summer plums
year-round with this very simple spread.**

2⅔ pounds firm, ripe red plums
(about 30 plums), halved,
pitted, and finely chopped

½ cup water

Cheesecloth

4 tablespoons Ball® Classic Pectin

3⅓ cups sugar

LOW SUGAR

Increase the plums to 4½ pounds
and water to ⅔ cup to collect
4⅔ cups plum juice. Substitute
4 tablespoons Ball® Low or
No-Sugar Needed Pectin for
the Classic Pectin and reduce
the sugar to 1 cup. This jelly
will have a looser set than the
full-sugar version, but even more
fresh fruit flavor.

❶ Bring the chopped plums and water to a boil in a 6-quart
stainless-steel or enameled Dutch oven. Cover; reduce heat, and
simmer 10 minutes.

❷ Pour the plum mixture through a mesh strainer lined with 3 layers
of dampened cheesecloth into a bowl. Let drain 2 to 4 hours or until
the juice measures 3 cups. (To avoid cloudy jelly, do not press or
squeeze the plum mixture.)

❸ Combine the plum juice and the pectin in a 6-quart stainless-
steel or enameled Dutch oven. Bring the mixture to a rolling boil
that cannot be stirred down, over high, stirring constantly.

❹ Add the sugar, stirring to dissolve. Return to a full rolling boil.
Boil hard 1 minute, stirring constantly. Remove from heat. Skim
the foam, if necessary.

❺ Ladle the hot jelly into a hot jar, leaving ¼-inch headspace.
Wipe the jar rim. Center the lid on the jar. Apply the band, and
adjust to fingertip-tight. Place the jar in the boiling water canner.
Repeat until all the jars are filled.

❻ Process the jars 10 minutes, adjusting for altitude. Turn off heat;
remove the lid, and let the jars stand 5 minutes. Remove the jars
and cool.

CHAMPAGNE JELLY

This elegant jelly combines the crisp flavor of raspberry with the sparkle of Champagne.

1 Combine the raspberry juice and the lemon juice in a large stainless-steel or enameled saucepan. Gradually stir in the pectin. Bring to a boil over high, stirring frequently. Add the sugar, and return to a full rolling boil that cannot be stirred down, stirring constantly. Boil hard for 1 minute, stirring constantly. Remove from heat. Stir in the Champagne. Skim the foam, if necessary.

2 Ladle the hot jelly into a hot jar, leaving ¼-inch headspace. Wipe the jar rim. Center the lid on the jar. Apply the band, and adjust to fingertip-tight. Place the jar in the boiling water canner. Repeat until all the jars are filled.

3 Process the jars 10 minutes, adjusting for altitude. Turn off heat; remove the lid, and let the jars stand 5 minutes. Remove the jars and cool.

3 cups bottled raspberry juice

¼ cup lemon juice

3 tablespoons Ball® Classic Pectin

4 cups sugar

1¼ cups Champagne

GRAPE JELLY

Treat yourself with this flavorful crowd-pleaser. Once you use homemade jelly in a classic PB&J, you may never go back.

1 Rinse the grapes under running water; drain. Crush the grapes, 1 layer at a time, with a potato masher in a 6-quart stainless-steel or enameled Dutch oven. Add the water, and bring to a boil. Cover; reduce heat, and simmer about 15 minutes.

2 Pour the grape mixture through a mesh strainer lined with 3 layers of dampened cheesecloth into a bowl. Let drain 2 to 4 hours or until the juice measures 3 cups. (To avoid cloudy jelly, do not press or squeeze the grape mixture.)

3 Combine the grape juice and the pectin in a 6-quart stainless-steel or enameled Dutch oven. Bring the mixture to a rolling boil that cannot be stirred down, over high, stirring constantly.

4 Add the sugar, stirring to dissolve. Return to a full rolling boil. Boil hard 1 minute, stirring constantly. Remove from heat. Skim the foam, if necessary.

5 Ladle the hot jelly into a hot jar, leaving ¼-inch headspace. Wipe the jar rim. Center the lid on the jar. Apply the band, and adjust to fingertip-tight. Place the jar in the boiling water canner. Repeat until all the jars are filled.

6 Process the jars 10 minutes, adjusting for altitude. Turn off heat; remove the lid, and let the jars stand 5 minutes. Remove the jars and cool.

2½ pounds Concord grapes

½ cup water

Cheesecloth

4 tablespoons Ball® Classic Pectin

3⅓ cups sugar

LOW SUGAR

Increase the grapes to 4 pounds and water to ⅔ cup to collect 4⅔ cups grape juice. Substitute 4 tablespoons Ball® Low or No-Sugar Needed Pectin for the Classic Pectin and reduce the sugar to 1 cup. This jelly will have a looser set than the full-sugar version, but even more fresh fruit flavor.

TIP

Save time by substituting a high-quality unsweetened bottled grape juice, and then go to step 3.

GUAVA–VANILLA BEAN JELLY

**Sunny yellow tropical guavas from Florida or Hawaii yield
juice that surprisingly turns into a pretty pink jelly. Excellent on toast,
it also doubles as a glaze for fruit desserts or grilled meats.**

1 Remove the ends of the guavas. Cut lengthwise into quarters, and then crosswise into thin slices. Combine the guava slices and the water in a 4-quart stainless-steel or enameled Dutch oven. Bring to a boil; reduce heat, cover, and simmer 20 minutes, stirring occasionally.

2 Pour the guava through a mesh strainer lined with 3 layers of dampened cheesecloth into a bowl. Let drain 2 hours or until the juice measures 4½ cups. (To avoid cloudy jelly, do not press or squeeze the guava.)

3 Scrape the seeds from the vanilla beans. Combine the vanilla bean seeds, vanilla beans, guava juice, pectin, and citrus juices in the same Dutch oven. Bring the mixture to a rolling boil that cannot be stirred down, over high, stirring constantly.

4 Add the sugar, stirring to dissolve. Return to a full rolling boil. Boil hard 1 minute, stirring constantly. Remove from heat. Skim the foam, if necessary.

5 Ladle the hot jelly into a hot jar, leaving ¼-inch headspace. Wipe the jar rim. Center the lid on the jar. Apply the band, and adjust to fingertip-tight. Place the jar in the boiling water canner. Repeat until all the jars are filled.

6 Process the jars 10 minutes, adjusting for altitude. Turn off heat; remove the lid, and let the jars stand 5 minutes. Remove the jars and cool.

4½ pounds guavas

5½ cups water

Cheesecloth

2 vanilla beans, split lengthwise

6 tablespoons Ball® Classic Pectin

1 tablespoon lemon juice

1 tablespoon fresh lime juice

3 cups sugar

APPLE JELLY

Choose sweet apple varieties such as Gala and Fuji, that produce lots of juice. Just as for applesauce, a variety of apples will make a more flavorful jelly.

2½ pounds apples

3 cups water

Cheesecloth

4 tablespoons Ball® Classic Pectin

3⅓ cups sugar

LOW SUGAR

Increase the apples to 4 pounds and water to 5 cups to collect 4⅔ cups apple juice. Substitute 4 tablespoons Ball® Low or No-Sugar Needed Pectin for the Classic Pectin and reduce the sugar to 1 cup. This jelly will have a looser set than the full-sugar version, but even more fresh fruit flavor.

❶ Rinse the apples under cold running water; pat dry. Stem and cut the apples into chunks (do not core). Bring the apples and water to a boil in a 6-quart stainless-steel or enameled Dutch oven. Cover; reduce heat, and simmer 10 minutes. Crush with a potato masher, and simmer 5 more minutes.

❷ Pour the apple mixture through a mesh strainer lined with 3 layers of dampened cheesecloth into a bowl. Let drain 2 to 4 hours or until the juice measures 3 cups. (To avoid cloudy jelly, do not press or squeeze the apple mixture.)

❸ Combine the apple juice and pectin in a 6-quart stainless-steel or enameled Dutch oven. Bring the mixture to a rolling boil that cannot be stirred down, over high, stirring constantly.

❹ Add the sugar, stirring to dissolve. Return to a full rolling boil. Boil hard 1 minute, stirring constantly. Remove from heat. Skim the foam, if necessary.

❺ Ladle the hot jelly into a hot jar, leaving ¼-inch headspace. Wipe the jar rim. Center the lid on the jar. Apply the band, and adjust to fingertip-tight. Place the jar in the boiling water canner. Repeat until all the jars are filled.

❻ Process the jars 10 minutes, adjusting for altitude. Turn off heat; remove the lid, and let the jars stand 5 minutes. Remove the jars and cool.

RHUBARB JELLY

MAKES ABOUT 5 (½-PINT) JARS

Choose dark red stalks for the best color in this spring jelly. Use it as the filling for a jelly-roll cake or to accompany pork roast.

❶ Combine the rhubarb and the water in a 6-quart stainless-steel or enameled Dutch oven. Bring to a boil; reduce heat, and simmer, uncovered, 20 minutes. Remove from heat. Skim the foam, if necessary.

❷ Pour the rhubarb mixture through a mesh strainer lined with 3 layers of dampened cheesecloth into a bowl. Let drain 2 hours or until the juice measures 4½ cups. (To avoid cloudy jelly, do not press or squeeze the rhubarb.)

❸ Wash the Dutch oven. Stir together the juice and the pectin in the same Dutch oven. Bring the mixture to a full rolling boil that cannot be stirred down, over high, stirring constantly.

❹ Add the sugar, stirring to dissolve. Return the mixture to a full rolling boil. Boil hard 1 minute, stirring constantly. Remove from heat. Skim the foam, if necessary.

❺ Ladle the hot jelly into a hot jar, leaving ¼-inch headspace. Wipe the jar rim. Center the lid on the jar. Apply the band, and adjust to fingertip-tight. Place the jar in the boiling water canner. Repeat until all the jars are filled.

❻ Process the jars 10 minutes, adjusting for altitude. Turn off heat; remove the lid, and let the jars stand 5 minutes. Remove the jars and cool.

3½ pounds rhubarb, trimmed and cut into ½-inch pieces (10 cups)

1 quart water

Cheesecloth

6 tablespoons Ball® Classic Pectin

6 cups sugar

JELLIES

TART MINT or BASIL JELLY

MAKES ABOUT 7 (½-PINT) JARS

Serve this versatile jelly alongside roast lamb or beef. Liquid pectin gives this recipe a softer set, which makes it easier to use in marinades and glazes.

6¼ cups sugar

2 cups water

1 cup white vinegar (5% acidity)

1 cup loosely packed fresh mint leaves, or 1½ cups loosely packed fresh basil leaves, rinsed, dried, bruised slightly, and tied in cheesecloth

1 to 6 drops of green liquid food coloring (optional)

2 (3-ounce) pouches Ball® Liquid Pectin

❶ Combine the first 4 ingredients and, if desired, food coloring, in a 6-quart stainless-steel or enameled Dutch oven. Bring the mixture to a full rolling boil that cannot be stirred down, over high, stirring frequently.

❷ Add the pectin, immediately squeezing entire contents from the pouches. Continue hard boil for 1 minute, stirring constantly. Remove from heat; remove and discard the mint and cheesecloth. Skim the foam, if necessary.

❸ Ladle the hot jelly into a hot jar, leaving ¼-inch headspace. Wipe the jar rim. Center the lid on the jar. Apply the band, and adjust to fingertip-tight. Place the jar in the boiling water canner. Repeat until all the jars are filled.

❹ Process the jars 10 minutes, adjusting for altitude. Turn off heat; remove the lid, and let the jars stand 5 minutes. Remove the jars and cool.

CHANGE IT UP

Make this with rosemary. Substitute ½ cup minced fresh rosemary leaves in place of the mint or basil, and leave out the food coloring. Use a small mesh strainer to remove the rosemary solids before filling the jars in step 3.

TART LEMON JELLY

MAKES ABOUT 4 (½-PINT) JARS

Tart and sweet, this jelly is a popular filling for doughnuts, jelly-roll cakes, and cookies.

6 large lemons (1½ pounds)

1½ cups water

Cheesecloth

3 tablespoons Ball® Classic Pectin

4 cups sugar

CHANGE IT UP

Make lime jelly! Follow the recipe exactly using lime juice and lime zest instead of lemon.

❶ Scrub the lemons thoroughly under cold running water; rinse well, and pat dry. Carefully remove the zest from the lemons with a vegetable peeler to measure 1 cup, avoiding the bitter white pith.

❷ Using a sharp, thin-bladed knife, cut a ¼-inch-thick slice from each end of the lemons. Place the lemons flat-end down on a cutting board, and remove and discard the peel (bitter white pith) in strips, cutting from top to bottom, and following the curvature of the fruit. Coarsely chop the lemons, reserving all the juice, to measure 4 cups.

❸ Combine the lemon zest, chopped lemon with reserved juice, and water in a 4-quart stainless-steel or enameled Dutch oven. Bring to a boil; reduce heat, cover, and simmer 15 minutes.

❹ Pour the lemon mixture through a mesh strainer lined with 3 layers of dampened cheesecloth into a bowl. Let drain at least 3 hours or overnight until the juice measures 2 cups. Discard the solids.

❺ Combine the lemon juice and the pectin in a 4-quart stainless-steel or enameled Dutch oven. Bring the mixture to a full rolling boil that cannot be stirred down, over high, stirring constantly.

❻ Add the sugar, stirring to dissolve. Return the mixture to a full rolling boil. Boil hard 1 minute, stirring constantly. Remove from heat. Skim the foam, if necessary.

❼ Ladle the hot jelly into a hot jar, leaving ¼-inch headspace. Wipe the jar rim. Center the lid on the jar. Apply the band, and adjust to fingertip-tight. Place the jar in the boiling water canner. Repeat until all the jars are filled.

❽ Process the jars 10 minutes, adjusting for altitude. Turn off heat; remove the lid, and let the jars stand 5 minutes. Remove the jars and cool.

PEPPER JELLY

MAKES ABOUT 6 (½-PINT) JARS

To make a super-fast appetizer, layer this on baked Brie and heat in the microwave. Serve with whole-grain crackers.

❶ Rinse the peppers under cold running water; drain. Remove the stems and the seeds. Process the peppers with 1 cup of the apple cider vinegar in a food processor or blender until smooth.

❷ Combine the green bell peppers, jalapeño peppers, and remaining vinegar in a large stainless-steel or enameled Dutch oven. Gradually add the pectin. Bring the mixture to a full rolling boil that cannot be stirred down, over high, stirring constantly.

❸ Add the sugar and the honey. Return the mixture to a full rolling boil. Boil hard 3 minutes, stirring constantly. Remove from heat. Skim the foam, if necessary.

❹ Ladle the hot jelly into a hot jar, leaving ¼-inch headspace. Wipe the jar rim. Center the lid on the jar. Apply the band, and adjust to fingertip-tight. Place the jar in the boiling water canner. Repeat until all the jars are filled.

❺ Process the jars 10 minutes, adjusting for altitude. Turn off heat; remove the lid, and let the jars stand 5 minutes. Remove the jars and cool.

4 ½ cups finely chopped green bell pepper (about 4 large)

½ cup finely chopped jalapeño pepper (about 4 small)

1 ¼ cups apple cider vinegar

3 tablespoons Ball® Low or No-Sugar Needed Pectin

2 cups sugar

1 cup honey

TIP

When cutting or seeding hot peppers, wear rubber gloves to prevent your hands from being burned. And be careful not to touch your eyes!

JELLIES

HABANERO-APRICOT JELLY

MAKES ABOUT 6 (½-PINT) JARS

**This beautiful jelly is great as a spicy-sweet glaze for
cooked shrimp or chicken wings, or stirred into mayonnaise
to punch up sandwich spreads and dips.**

1 Combine the vinegar and apricots in a medium bowl. Cover and let stand at room temperature at least 4 hours or overnight.

2 Stir together the apricot mixture, sugar, and next 3 ingredients in a 6-quart stainless-steel or enameled Dutch oven. Bring the mixture to a full rolling boil that cannot be stirred down, over high, stirring frequently.

3 Add the pectin, immediately squeezing entire contents from the pouch. Boil hard for 1 minute, stirring constantly. Remove from heat. Skim the foam, if necessary.

4 Ladle the hot jelly into a hot jar, leaving ¼-inch headspace. Wipe the jar rim. Center the lid on the jar. Apply the band, and adjust to fingertip-tight. Place the jar in the boiling water canner. Repeat until all the jars are filled.

5 Process the jars 10 minutes, adjusting for altitude. Turn off heat; remove the lid, and let the jars stand 5 minutes. Remove the jars and cool.

1½ cups white vinegar (5% acidity)

⅔ cup finely chopped dried apricots

6 cups sugar

½ cup finely chopped red bell pepper

½ cup finely chopped red onion

¼ cup finely chopped seeded habanero pepper

1 (3-ounce) pouch Ball® Liquid Pectin

3

FRUIT

Savor the season year-round by preserving whole or sliced fruit at the peak of ripeness. You can pack the fruit in sugar syrup, fruit juice, or water depending on your preference. But sugar syrup helps in retaining the texture, color, and flavor of the fruit. Peaches, strawberries, and cherries are especially succulent when canned this way. Get creative by adding dry spices to any of these recipes.

HOW TO CAN FRUIT

You will need:

- Tested recipe and ingredients
- Glass preserving jars with lids and bands (always start with new lids)
- Water bath canner or a large, deep stockpot with lid and rack
- Jar lifter
- Common kitchen utensils, including measuring cups and spoons, large ladle, kitchen towel, and rubber spatula
- Large stainless-steel or enameled saucepan or Dutch oven
- Bubble remover and headspace measuring tool
- Labels

TIPS

Choose fruit that is bruise- and blemish-free at the peak of freshness.

You may also use a dishwasher to wash and heat the jars.

STEP 1: HEAT JARS Examine the jars for defects. Place a canning rack at the bottom of the canner and fill halfway with water. Place the jars in and bring the water almost to a simmer over medium. **IMPORTANT:** Keep the jars hot until ready to fill to prevent jar breakage. Wash lids and bands in warm soapy water, rinse, and set aside.

STEP 2: PREP Prepare the chosen fruit according to the recipe. Prepare the syrup, if using, according to the chart (page 98). Bring the sugar, or alternate sweetener, and water to a boil in a stainless-steel saucepan, stirring to dissolve. Reduce heat; cover and keep hot until needed. (Do not allow the liquid to evaporate.)

RAW PACK

STEP 3: COOK Raw Pack is faster and generally used for more delicate fruit. Bring the syrup, juice, or water to a simmer in a stainless-steel or enameled saucepan. Cover and keep warm until needed.

STEP 4: FILL Working with one hot jar at a time, pack the fruit in overlapping layers in the jar. Ladle hot syrup over the fruit, leaving required headspace. Remove air bubbles. Wipe the jar rim. Center the lid on the jar. Apply the band and adjust to fingertip-tight. Place the jar in the boiling water canner. Repeat until all the jars are filled.

HOT PACK

STEP 3: COOK Hot Pack requires cooking the fruit before it goes into the jars. This helps break down the fruit before canning. Bring the syrup, juice, or water to a simmer in a Dutch oven. Add the fruit, 1 layer at a time, and simmer in the hot liquid until thoroughly heated.

STEP 4: FILL Working with one hot jar at a time, pack the fruit in overlapping layers in the jar. Ladle the hot liquid over the fruit, leaving ½-inch headspace. Remove air bubbles. Wipe the jar rim. Center the lid on the jar. Apply the band and adjust to fingertip-tight.

STEP 5: Place the filled jar in the boiling water canner. Repeat one at a time until all the jars are filled. (If using a canning rack, lower the rack with the jars into the water.) Make sure the water covers the jars by at least 1 inch. Add more hot water if needed.

STEP 6: PROCESS Place the lid on the canner and bring the water to a full rolling boil. Process the jars 10 to 25 minutes according to the recipe (adjusting for altitude, page 16). Maintain a rolling boil throughout the entire processing period. Turn off heat and remove the lid. Let the canner cool 5 minutes before removing the jars.

STEP 7: Using the jar lifter, remove the jars from the canner and set upright on a towel or cutting board, leaving at least 2 inches between the jars. Leave undisturbed for at least 12 hours. The bands may loosen during processing but should not be retightened, as this may interfere with the sealing process.

STEP 8: TEST & STORE Check the lids for vacuum seals after stand time. The lids should not flex up and down when the center is pressed. Remove the bands. Gently try to lift off the lid with your fingertips. If the lid cannot be lifted off, the lid has a good seal. Wipe the jars and lids with a clean, damp cloth. Label and store in a cool, dry, dark place up to 1 year.

FRUIT

Syrups for Canning Fruit

SYRUP TYPE	SELECTION	% SUGAR	ALTERNATE SWEETENER	SUGAR	WATER	YIELD*
Super-Light	Approximates natural sugar level in most fruits.	10		½ cup	5 cups	5¼ cups
Extra-Light	Use with very sweet fruit.	20		1½ cups	5¾ cups	6 cups
Light	Use with sweet apples; dark, sweet cherries; berries; and grapes.	30		2¼ cups	5¼ cups	6½ cups
Medium	Use with tart apples; apricots; tart, red cherries; gooseberries; nectarines; peaches; pears; and plums.	40		3¼ cups	5 cups	7 cups
Heavy	Use with very sour fruit.	50		4¼ cups	4¼ cups	7 cups
Honey			1 cup		4 cups	5 cups

*Each 1 (1-quart) jar of fruit requires about 1 to 1½ cups syrup.

Dry Spices

Dry spices don't affect the pH of your preserved fruit in any way so feel free to add them to these recipes for an extra flavor twist. Here are some spices that pair well with many fruits in this chapter:

Cinnamon sticks
Crystallized ginger
Nutmeg

Cloves
Allspice
Vanilla beans

Cardamom
Dried thyme, oregano, rosemary, or culinary lavender

STRAWBERRIES

Preserved strawberries have a different texture than fresh, but are equally wonderful served over pancakes, waffles, or shortcakes.

6 pounds firm, ripe strawberries, hulled

Sugar

❶ Rinse the strawberries under cold running water; drain and place in a large glass bowl. For each quart of strawberries, add ½ to ¾ cup sugar, stirring well. Cover and let stand in a cool place 5 hours.

❷ Transfer the strawberry mixture to a 6-quart stainless-steel or enameled Dutch oven. Slowly bring to a boil; reduce heat, and simmer, uncovered, just until thoroughly heated and the sugar dissolves, stirring gently to prevent sticking.

❸ Pack the hot strawberry mixture into a hot jar, leaving ½-inch headspace. Remove air bubbles. Wipe the jar rim. Center the lid on the jar. Apply the band, and adjust to fingertip-tight. Place the jar in the boiling water canner. Repeat until all the jars are filled.

❹ Process 1-pint jars 10 minutes, or 1-quart jars 15 minutes, adjusting for altitude. Turn off heat; remove the lid, and let the jars stand 5 minutes. Remove the jars and cool.

CRANBERRIES

MAKES ABOUT 4 (1-PINT) JARS OR 2 (1-QUART) JARS

Use only fresh cranberries for preserving.

3 pounds firm fresh cranberries, stemmed

3 cups Heavy Syrup for Canning Fruit (page 98)

❶ Rinse the cranberries under cold running water; drain.

❷ Bring the cranberries and the syrup to a simmer in a 6-quart stainless-steel or enameled Dutch oven. Cook 3 minutes.

❸ Pack the cranberries into a hot jar. Ladle the hot syrup over the berries, leaving ½-inch headspace. Remove air bubbles. Wipe the jar rim. Center the lid on the jar. Apply the band, and adjust to fingertip-tight. Place the jar in the boiling water canner. Repeat until all the jars are filled.

❹ Process 1-pint or 1-quart jars 15 minutes, adjusting for altitude. Turn off heat; remove the lid, and let the jars stand 5 minutes. Remove the jars and cool.

BERRIES

Use this recipe to preserve blueberries, currants, raspberries, and elderberries.

❶ Rinse the berries under cold running water; drain.

RAW PACK: (Use with raspberries or other berries that don't hold their shape when heated.): Bring the syrup to a simmer in a stainless-steel or enameled saucepan. Cover and keep warm until needed. Pack the berries gently in a hot jar (do not crush). Ladle the hot syrup over the berries, leaving ½-inch headspace. Remove air bubbles. Wipe the jar rim. Center the lid on the jar. Apply the band and adjust to fingertip-tight. Place the jar in the boiling water canner. Repeat until all the jars are filled.

HOT PACK: For each 1 quart of berries, combine the berries and ¼ to ½ cup sugar in a glass bowl. Cover and let stand in a cool place 2 hours. Transfer the berry mixture to a 6-quart stainless-steel or enameled Dutch oven. Cook over medium-low until thoroughly heated and the sugar dissolves, stirring occasionally to prevent sticking. Ladle the berry mixture into a hot jar, leaving ½-inch headspace. Remove air bubbles. Wipe the jar rim. Center the lid on the jar. Apply the band, and adjust to fingertip-tight. Place the jar in the boiling water canner. Repeat until all the jars are filled.

❷ Process 1-pint or 1-quart jars 15 minutes, adjusting for altitude. Turn off heat; remove the lid, and let the jars stand 5 minutes. Remove the jars and cool.

3 to 6 pounds firm ripe berries

3 cups Extra-Light or Light Syrup for Canning Fruit (page 98)

Sugar (for Hot Pack)

FRUIT

RHUBARB

MAKES ABOUT 4 (1-PINT) JARS OR 2 (1-QUART) JARS

The pleasing tartness of rhubarb works perfectly in pies and tarts.

4 pounds young, tender, colorful rhubarb stalks

Sugar

❶ Rinse the rhubarb under cold running water. Trim and discard any leafy tops; cut into 1-inch slices, and place in a large glass bowl. For each quart of rhubarb slices, add ½ to 1 cup sugar, stirring well. Cover and let stand in a cool place 4 hours, stirring occasionally until juice appears.

❷ Transfer to a 6-quart stainless-steel or enameled Dutch oven. Slowly bring the rhubarb to a boil, stirring to prevent sticking; boil 30 seconds.

❸ Pack the hot rhubarb and the juice into a hot jar, leaving ½-inch headspace. Remove air bubbles. Wipe the jar rim. Center the lid on the jar. Apply the band, and adjust to fingertip-tight. Place the jar in the boiling water canner. Repeat until all the jars are filled.

❹ Process 1-pint or 1-quart jars 15 minutes, adjusting for altitude. Turn off heat; remove the lid, and let the jars stand 5 minutes. Remove the jars and cool.

PINEAPPLE

**Home-canned pineapple is wonderfully versatile
and has a far superior flavor to commercially canned.**

5 pounds ripe pineapple, scrubbed and peeled, eyes removed

3 cups Extra-Light or Light Syrup for Canning (page 98)

❶ Core the pineapple with a pineapple corer. Cut into ½-inch slices or 1-inch chunks. Bring the syrup to a simmer in a 6-quart stainless-steel or enameled Dutch oven. Add the pineapple (1 layer at a time for slices); cook until thoroughly heated. Pack the pineapple in a hot jar.

❷ Ladle the hot syrup over the fruit, leaving ½-inch headspace. Remove air bubbles. Wipe the jar rim. Center the lid on the jar. Apply the band, and adjust to fingertip-tight. Place the jar in the boiling water canner. Repeat until all the jars are filled.

❸ Process 1-pint jars 15 minutes, or 1-quart jars 20 minutes, adjusting for altitude. Turn off heat: remove the lid, and let the jars stand 5 minutes. Remove the jars and cool.

TIP

Wide mouth jars are best for the pineapple rings. If you don't have a pineapple corer, cut the pineapple into slices. Remove the centers of the slices with the removable center of a donut cutter or a ¾- to 1-inch biscuit cutter.

FRUIT SALAD

MAKES ABOUT 6 (1-PINT) JARS OR 3 (1-QUART) JARS

Try different fruit combinations to customize your own homemade fruit cocktail.

6 to 9 pounds mixed fruit (apricots, cherries, grapefruit, peaches, pears, pineapple, plums, white grapes, etc.)

1 batch Extra-Light or Light Syrup for Canning Fruit (page 98)

1. Use 3 or more varieties of fruit. Rinse under cold running water; drain. Prep as instructed for individual fruit type. Peel, halve, and pit apricots and peaches. Halve and pit plums. Peel and core pineapples. Cut into ½-inch cubes. Halve and pit cherries. Add seedless grapes whole.

2. Prepare the syrup for canning in a large stainless-steel or enameled saucepan. Bring the mixture to a boil over medium-high. Cook the fruit in syrup until hot throughout.

3. Pack the hot fruit into a hot jar, leaving ½-inch headspace. Ladle the hot syrup over the fruit, leaving ½-inch headspace. Remove air bubbles. Wipe the jar rim. Center the lid on the jar. Apply the band, and adjust to fingertip-tight. Place the jar in the boiling water canner. Repeat until all the jars are filled.

4. Process 1-pint or 1-quart jars 20 minutes, adjusting for altitude. Turn off heat; remove the lid, and let the jars stand 5 minutes. Remove the jars and cool.

CHANGE IT UP

Pack these in easy to-go lunch-friendly sizes. Use 4-ounce jars and reduce the process time to 15 minutes, adjusting for altitude.

CHERRIES

MAKES ABOUT 4 (1-PINT) JARS OR 2 (1-QUART) JARS

Head to your local farmers' market for fresh tart cherries.

① Rinse the cherries in cold running water; drain. Pit the cherries, if desired. (Prick skins of unpitted cherries on opposite sides with a needle to reduce splitting.)

RAW PACK: Bring the syrup to a simmer in a stainless-steel or enameled saucepan. Cover and keep warm until needed. Pack the fruit gently into a hot jar (do not crush). Ladle the hot syrup over the fruit, leaving ½-inch headspace. Remove air bubbles. Wipe the jar rim. Center the lid on the jar. Apply the band, and adjust to fingertip-tight. Place the jar in the boiling water canner. Repeat until all the jars are filled. Process 1-pint or 1-quart jars 25 minutes, adjusting for altitude.

HOT PACK: For each 1 quart of fruit, combine the cherries and ½ to ¾ cup sugar in a 6-quart stainless-steel or enameled Dutch oven. Cook over medium-low until thoroughly heated, stirring until the sugar dissolves. (Add just enough water to the unpitted cherries to prevent sticking.) Ladle the cherries and juice into a hot jar, leaving ½-inch headspace. Remove air bubbles. Wipe the jar rim. Center the lid on the jar. Apply the band, and adjust to fingertip-tight. Place the jar in the boiling water canner. Repeat until all the jars are filled. Process 1-pint jars 15 minutes, or 1-quart jars 20 minutes, adjusting for altitude.

② Turn off heat; remove the lid, and let the jars stand 5 minutes. Remove the jars and cool.

5 pounds sweet or tart cherries, stemmed

3 cups Light (for sweet cherries), or Medium or Heavy (for tart cherries) Syrup for Canning Fruit (page 98)

Sugar (for Hot Pack)

CHANGE IT UP

Almonds and cinnamon are two flavors that pair well with cherries. Add a teaspoon of almond extract to the syrup, or place a cinnamon stick in each jar for extra flavor.

FRUIT

BRANDIED CHERRIES

These gorgeous cherries make perfect homemade gifts. Use them in cocktails, or over pound cake or ice cream.

1. Rinse the cherries under cold running water; drain. Stem and pit the cherries.

2. Combine the sugar, water, and lemon juice in a large stainless-steel or enameled saucepan. Bring the mixture to a boil, stirring until the sugar dissolves. Reduce heat to a simmer (180°F). Add the cherries and simmer until they are hot throughout. Remove the saucepan from heat. Stir in the brandy.

3. Pack the hot cherries into a hot jar, leaving ½-inch headspace. Ladle the hot syrup over the cherries, leaving ½-inch headspace. Remove air bubbles. Wipe the jar rim. Center the lid on the jar. Apply the band, and adjust to fingertip-tight. Place the jar on the rack elevated over simmering water (180°F) in the boiling water canner. Repeat until all the jars are filled.

4. Lower the rack into simmering water. Water must cover jars by 1 inch. Adjust heat to medium-high, cover the canner, and bring the water to a rolling boil.

5. Process the jars 10 minutes, adjusting for altitude. Turn off heat; remove the lid, and let the jars stand 5 minutes. Remove the jars and cool.

6 pounds dark sweet cherries

1 cup sugar

1 cup water

½ cup bottled lemon juice

1¼ cups brandy

PLUMS

Add chopped plums to quick breads and muffins, or on top of your morning yogurt.

4 pounds firm, ripe plums

3 cups Medium or Heavy Syrup for Canning Fruit (page 98)

❶ Rinse the plums under cold running water; pat dry. Halve and pit the plums. Bring the syrup to a simmer in a 6-quart stainless-steel or enameled Dutch oven. Add the plum halves; cook 5 minutes. Remove from heat and let stand 30 minutes. Transfer the plums to a glass bowl with a slotted spoon; return the syrup to a boil.

❷ Pack the plums into a hot jar, and ladle the hot syrup over the fruit, leaving ½-inch headspace. Remove air bubbles. Wipe the jar rim. Center the lid on the jar. Apply the band, and adjust to fingertip-tight. Place the jar in the boiling water canner. Repeat until all the jars are filled.

❸ Process 1-pint jars 20 minutes, or 1-quart jars 25 minutes, adjusting for altitude. Turn off heat; remove the lid, and let the jars stand 5 minutes. Remove the jars and cool.

APRICOTS

Enjoy these delicious sweet treats right out of the jar, baked on top of a coffee cake, or as a quick filling for a galette.

① Rinse the apricots under cold running water; pat dry. Halve and pit the apricots.

RAW PACK: Bring the syrup, juice, or water to a simmer in a stainless-steel or enameled saucepan. Cover and keep warm until needed. Pack the apricot halves, cavity side down, in overlapping layers in a hot jar. Ladle the hot syrup over the fruit, leaving ½-inch headspace. Remove air bubbles. Wipe the jar rim. Center the lid on the jar. Apply the band, and adjust to fingertip-tight. Place the jar in the boiling water canner. Repeat until all the jars are filled.

HOT PACK: Bring the syrup, juice, or water to a simmer in a 6-quart stainless-steel or enameled Dutch oven. Add the apricot halves, 1 layer at a time, and simmer in the hot liquid until thoroughly heated. Pack, cavity side down, in overlapping layers in a hot jar. Ladle the hot liquid over the fruit, leaving ½-inch headspace. Remove air bubbles. Wipe the jar rim. Center the lid on the jar. Apply the band, and adjust to fingertip-tight. Place the jar in the boiling water canner. Repeat until all the jars are filled.

② Process 1-pint jars 20 minutes, or 1-quart jars 25 minutes, adjusting for altitude. Turn off heat; remove the lid, and let the jars stand 5 minutes. Remove the jars and cool.

5 pounds ripe apricots

3 cups Extra-Light, Light, or Medium Syrup for Canning Fruit (page 98), juice, or water

DRUNKEN PEACHES

MAKES ABOUT 6 (1-PINT) JARS

Sweet vanilla-flavored syrup spiked with bourbon helps create a decadent and elegant dessert topping for vanilla ice cream or other fruit in a compote.

1 lemon

5 pounds fresh firm, ripe freestone peaches

3 cups water

2½ cups sugar

3 vanilla beans, halved crosswise

6 (¼-inch-thick) orange slices (from 2 small navel oranges)

¾ cup bourbon

❶ Rinse the lemon and peaches under cold running water; pat dry. Bring a large pot of water to a boil. Fill a large bowl two-thirds full of ice water. Cut the lemon in half, and squeeze the juice into the ice water. Working in batches, place the peaches in a wire basket, lower into the boiling water, and blanch 1 minute. Place immediately in the lemon juice mixture. When cool enough to handle, peel the peaches, cut in half, and remove the pits. Cut each half into 4 wedges; return to the lemon juice mixture.

❷ Stir together 3 cups water and the sugar in a large stainless-steel or enameled saucepan. Split the vanilla bean halves lengthwise; scrape out the seeds. Add the vanilla bean and seeds to the sugar mixture; cook over medium-high, stirring until the sugar dissolves. Bring to and maintain at a low simmer.

❸ Place 1 orange slice and 1 vanilla bean half into a hot jar. Drain and tightly pack the peach quarters into the jar. Ladle the hot syrup into the jar, leaving 1½-inch headspace. Add 2 tablespoons bourbon to the jar. Add more hot syrup to the jar, leaving ½-inch headspace. Remove air bubbles. Wipe the jar rim. Center the lid on the jar. Apply the band, and adjust to fingertip-tight. Place the jar in the boiling water canner. Repeat until all the jars are filled.

❹ Process the jars 25 minutes, adjusting for altitude. Turn off heat; remove the lid, and let the jars stand 5 minutes. Remove the jars and cool.

APPLES

**It's important to choose apple varieties that will hold
their shape nicely after cooking. For best results, choose firm
ripe apples, such as Granny Smith or Gala.**

4 to 6 pounds apples, rinsed, peeled, and cored

Ball® Fruit-Fresh® Produce Protector or lemon juice

3 cups Light or Medium Syrup for Canning Fruit (page 98)

❶ Cut the apples into halves, quarters, or ¼-inch slices. Treat with Ball® Fruit-Fresh® Produce Protector according to package directions.

❷ Bring the syrup to a boil in a 6-quart stainless-steel or enameled Dutch oven. Drain the apples; add to the syrup. Return to a simmer and cook 5 minutes, gently stirring occasionally until the apples are thoroughly heated.

❸ Pack the hot apples in a hot jar. Ladle the hot syrup over the apples, leaving ½-inch headspace. Remove air bubbles. Wipe the jar rim. Center the lid on the jar. Apply the band, and adjust to fingertip-tight. Place the jar in the boiling water canner. Repeat until all the jars are filled.

❹ Process 1-pint or 1-quart jars 20 minutes, adjusting for altitude. Turn off heat; remove the lid, and let the jars stand 5 minutes. Remove the jars and cool.

. . . . . .
CHANGE IT UP

Add a warming kick to your canned apples: Include a cinnamon stick and a few whole cloves to each jar. Using whole spices instead of ground will keep your syrup clear.
. . . . . .

BACK TO BASICS

HOMEMADE APPLE PIE FILLING

Spoon on top of a coffee cake or bake inside a galette.

❶ Bring sliced apples and sugar to a boil in large saucepan; reduce heat, and simmer, uncovered, 5 minutes, stirring often. Remove from heat, and stir in the juice and flavorings.

❷ Ladle the hot fruit mixture into a hot jar, leaving ½-inch headspace. Remove air bubbles. Wipe the jar rim. Center the lid on the jar. Apply the band, and adjust to fingertip-tight. Place the jar in the boiling water canner.

❸ Process the jar 30 minutes, adjusting for altitude. Turn off heat; remove the lid, and let the jar stand 5 minutes. Remove the jar and cool.

2 pounds apples, peeled, cored, and sliced ¼ inch thick (about 6 cups)

½ cup sugar

2 tablespoons lemon juice

½ teaspoon ground cinnamon

¼ teaspoon ground nutmeg

TIP

Before using fruit pie filling straight from the pantry, you'll want to thicken it. Drain ⅓ cup liquid from 1 jar of Homemade Apple Pie Filling into a medium saucepan. Whisk 3 tablespoons cornstarch into the liquid until smooth. Add the remaining contents of the jar to the cornstarch mixture, and stir gently to blend. Bring to a boil over medium-high. Reduce heat and simmer 1 minute.

PEACHES *of* NECTARINES

MAKES ABOUT 4 (1-PINT) JARS OR 2 (1-QUART) JARS

You can bake these into desserts, or drain and blend them with yogurt and ice for an easy smoothie.

5 pounds firm, ripe peaches or nectarines

Ball® Fruit-Fresh® Produce Protector or lemon juice

3 cups Light or Medium Syrup for Canning Fruit (page 98)

❶ Rinse the fruit under cold running water; pat dry. Peel the peaches (leave the nectarines unpeeled). Halve and pit the fruit; cut into slices, if desired. Treat with Ball® Fruit-Fresh® Produce Protector according to package directions.

RAW PACK: Bring the syrup to a simmer in a stainless-steel or enameled saucepan. Cover and keep warm until needed. Pack the fruit halves, cavity side down, in overlapping layers, into a hot jar. Ladle the hot syrup over the fruit, leaving ½-inch headspace. Remove air bubbles. Wipe the jar rim. Center the lid on the jar. Apply the band, and adjust to fingertip-tight. Place the jar in the boiling water canner. Repeat until all the jars are filled. Process 1-pint jars 25 minutes, or 1-quart jars 30 minutes, adjusting for altitude.

HOT PACK: Bring the syrup to a simmer in a 6-quart stainless-steel or enameled Dutch oven. Simmer the fruit halves, 1 layer at a time, in the syrup until thoroughly heated. Pack the halves, cavity side down, in overlapping layers in a hot jar. Ladle the hot syrup over the fruit, leaving ½-inch headspace. Remove the air bubbles. Wipe the jar rim. Center the lid on the jar. Apply the band, and adjust to fingertip-tight. Place the jar in the boiling water canner. Repeat until all the jars are filled. Process 1-pint jars 20 minutes, or 1-quart jars 25 minutes, adjusting for altitude.

❷ Turn off heat; remove the lid, and let the jars stand 5 minutes. Remove the jars and cool.

PEARS

MAKES ABOUT 4 (1-PINT) JARS OR 2 (1-QUART) JARS

Pears need to be ripe, but still firm, or they won't stand up to cooking.

1 Rinse the pears under cold running water; pat dry. Peel the pears; cut in half, and core using a melon baller or small spoon. Treat with Ball® Fruit-Fresh® Produce Protector according to package directions.

2 Bring the syrup to a simmer in a 6-quart stainless-steel or enameled Dutch oven. Drain the pears; add to the syrup, 1 layer at a time, and simmer, gently stirring occasionally, until the pears are thoroughly heated.

3 Pack the hot halves, cavity side down, in overlapping layers in a hot jar. Ladle the hot syrup over the halves, leaving ½-inch headspace. Remove air bubbles. Wipe the jar rim. Center the lid on the jar. Apply the band, and adjust to fingertip-tight. Place the jar in the boiling water canner. Repeat until all the jars are filled.

4 Process 1-pint jars 20 minutes, or 1-quart jars 25 minutes, adjusting for altitude. Turn off heat; remove the lid, and let the jars stand 5 minutes. Remove the jars and cool.

5 pounds firm, ripe pears

Ball® Fruit-Fresh® Produce Protector

3 cups Light or Medium Syrup for Canning Fruit (page 98)

FRUIT

HOMEMADE SWEET CHERRY PIE FILLING

MAKES 1 (1-QUART) JAR FILLING FOR 1 (9-INCH) PIE

Select bright, fully-ripe sweet dark cherries, such as Bing.

❶ Bring cherries and sugar to a boil in a large stainless-steel or enameled saucepan; reduce heat, and simmer, uncovered, 5 minutes, stirring often. Remove from heat, and stir in the juice and flavorings.

❷ Ladle the hot fruit mixture into a hot jar, leaving ½-inch headspace. Remove air bubbles. Wipe the jar rim. Center the lid on the jar. Apply the band, and adjust to fingertip-tight. Place the jar in the boiling water canner.

❸ Process the jar 30 minutes, adjusting for altitude. Turn off heat; remove the lid, and let the jar stand 5 minutes. Remove the jar and cool.

2 pounds dark, sweet cherries, stemmed, pitted, and chopped (about 6 cups)

½ cup sugar

2 tablespoons lemon juice

½ teaspoon ground cinnamon

¼ teaspoon almond extract

. . . . . .
TIP

Before using fruit pie filling straight from the pantry, you'll want to thicken it. Drain ⅓ cup liquid from 1 jar of Homemade Sweet Cherry Pie Filling into a medium saucepan. Whisk 3 tablespoons cornstarch into the liquid until smooth. Add the remaining contents of the jar to the cornstarch mixture, and stir gently to blend. Bring to a boil over medium-high. Reduce heat and simmer 1 minute.
. . . . . .

4

····

FRUIT BUTTERS *and* SAUCES

These rich, lush spreads are full of concentrated flavor.
Cooking down mashed fruit, sweetener, and seasonings long
and slow melds them in perfect balance, creating a thick, smooth
texture. These recipes are a great way to experiment with
flavorings such as star anise, cinnamon, nutmeg, ginger, or
even dry sherry or wine. Start with a small amount to
taste, and then go ahead and get adventurous!

HOW TO MAKE FRUIT BUTTERS

You will need:

- Tested recipe and ingredients
- Glass preserving jars with lids and bands (always start with new lids)
- Water bath canner or a large, deep stockpot with lid and rack
- Jar lifter
- Common kitchen utensils, including measuring cups and spoons, large ladle, kitchen towel, and rubber spatula
- Large stainless-steel or enameled saucepan or Dutch oven
- Canning funnel
- Bubble remover and headspace measuring tool
- Labels

TIPS

You may also use a dishwasher to wash and heat the jars.

If you don't have a food mill, you can also prepare the fruit by using a food processor, blender, or potato masher, and pass the mixture through a mesh strainer.

Fruit butters are cooked until they mound on a spoon. To test for doneness, put a small dollop of fruit butter onto a plate. If there is no separation of liquid from the fruit pulp, it's ready.

STEP 1: HEAT JARS Examine jars for defects. Place a canning rack at the bottom of canner and fill halfway with water. Place jars in and bring water almost to a simmer over medium. **IMPORTANT:** Keep jars hot until ready to fill to prevent breakage due to thermal shock. Wash lids and bands in warm soapy water, rinse, and set aside.

STEP 2: PREP INGREDIENTS Prepare the chosen fruit according to the recipe. Choose 1 liquid, 1 sweetener, and 1 seasoning from the **Liquids, Sweeteners, and Seasonings for Fruit Butter** chart (page 124).

STEP 3: COOK Combine fruit and lemon juice, if using, in a Dutch oven. Bring mixture to a boil; reduce heat, cover, and simmer until soft. Puree in a food mill. Return to Dutch oven; stir in desired liquid and flavorings. Bring to a boil; reduce heat, and simmer, uncovered, until thick and spreadable, stirring often.

STEP 4: FILL Using a ladle and canning funnel, fill a hot jar with the hot fruit mixture, leaving ½-inch headspace.

Remove air bubbles by sliding a bubble remover between the jar and food to release trapped air. Repeat around jar 2 or 3 times, and wipe the rim and top of the jar with a clean, damp cloth to remove any food residue, which can prevent a vacuum seal.

STEP 5: Center the lid on the jar, allowing sealing compound to come in contact with the jar rim. Apply the band and adjust until fit is fingertip-tight. Make sure the band is not overtightened—air inside the jars must be able to escape during canning.

STEP 6: Repeat one at a time until all the jars are filled. Place the filled jar in the canner. (If using a canning rack, lower the rack with the jars into the water.) Make sure the water covers the jars by at least 1 inch. Add more hot water if needed.

STEP 7: PROCESS Place the lid on the canner and bring the water to a full rolling boil. Once the water is fully boiling, set the timer to process the jars 10 minutes (adjusting for altitude, page 16). Maintain a rolling boil throughout the entire processing period. Turn off the heat and remove the lid. Let the canner cool 5 minutes before removing the jars.

STEP 8: Using the jar lifter, remove the jars from the canner and set upright on a towel or cutting board, leaving at least 2 inches between the jars. Leave undisturbed for at least 12 hours. The bands may loosen during processing but should not be retightened, as this may interfere with the sealing process.

STEP 9: TEST & STORE Check the lids for vacuum seals after stand time. Lids should not flex up and down when the center is pressed. Remove the bands. Gently try to lift off the lid with your fingertips. If the lid cannot be lifted off, the jar has a good seal. Wipe the jars and lids with a clean, damp cloth. Label and store in a cool, dry, dark place up to 1 year.

FRUIT BUTTERS and SAUCES

Liquids, Sweeteners, and Seasonings for Fruit Butter

Choose 1 liquid, 1 sweetener, and 1 seasoning (or a combination) from the chart below.

LIQUID	SWEETENER	SEASONING
¾ CUP	1 TO 2 CUPS*	TO TASTE
Apple cider	Agave nectar	Balsamic vinegar
Apple juice	Brown sugar	Citrus zest
Cranberry juice	Sugar	Dry sherry
Orange juice	Honey	Ground allspice
Pineapple juice	Maple syrup	Ground cinnamon
Water		Ground ginger
		Liqueur
		Star anise
		Vanilla extract

*Start with 1 cup sweetener. If desired, gradually add more to taste up to 2 cups.

How to Make Fruit Butter in a Slow Cooker

Combine the desired prepared fruit and lemon juice in a slow cooker. Cover and cook on HIGH 1 hour or until the fruit is very soft. Puree, in batches, in a food mill, food processor, or blender until smooth; stir in the desired liquid, sweetener, and spices, and return to the slow cooker. Partially cover and cook on HIGH until the mixture is thick and holds its shape on a spoon (about 6 to 10 hours), stirring occasionally. If desired, cook, partially covered, on LOW 8 hours or overnight. Fill the jars and process according to the instructions in each recipe.

PEACH BUTTER

**This recipe works with peaches or nectarines, or you can choose to
use a combination. Try vanilla or amaretto as flavorings.**

❶ Halve, pit, and chop the peaches. Bring the peaches and the
lemon juice to a boil in a 6-quart stainless-steel or enameled Dutch
oven; reduce heat, cover, and simmer until very soft. Remove from
heat. Let cool slightly. Process, in batches, in a food processor, food
mill, or blender until smooth.

❷ Return the peach mixture to the Dutch oven; stir in the desired
liquid, sweetener, and seasoning, beginning with 1 cup sweetener.
(If desired, gradually add more sweetener to taste, up to 2 cups.)

❸ Cook at a gentle boil over medium until the peach mixture
thickens and holds its shape on a spoon, stirring frequently to
prevent sticking. Remove from heat.

❹ Ladle the hot mixture into a hot jar, leaving ½-inch headspace.
Remove air bubbles. Wipe the jar rim. Center the lid on the jar.
Apply the band, and adjust to fingertip-tight. Place the jar in the
boiling water canner. Repeat until all the jars are filled.

❺ Process ½-pint and 1-pint jars 10 minutes, adjusting for altitude.
Turn off heat; remove the lid, and let the jars stand 5 minutes.
Remove the jars and cool.

6 pounds peaches (18 to 24
medium), rinsed and peeled, or
nectarines, rinsed and halved

¼ cup lemon juice

Liquid, Sweetener, and Seasoning,
as desired from chart (page 124)

APRICOT BUTTER

MAKES ABOUT 6 (½-PINT) JARS OR 3 (1-PINT) JARS

Dry sherry and nutmeg are good flavoring choices for this spread. Try serving it with cheese and crisp crackers.

4 ½ pounds apricots (about 35 medium), rinsed and halved

¼ cup lemon juice

Liquid, Sweetener, and Seasoning, as desired from chart (page 124)

❶ Pit and chop the apricots. Bring the apricots and the lemon juice to a boil in a 6-quart stainless-steel or enameled Dutch oven; reduce heat, cover, and simmer until very soft. Remove from heat. Let cool slightly. Process, in batches, in a food processor, food mill, or blender until smooth.

❷ Return the apricot mixture to the Dutch oven; stir in the desired liquid, sweetener, and seasoning, beginning with 1 cup sweetener. (If desired, gradually add more sweetener to taste, up to 2 cups.)

❸ Cook at a gentle boil over medium until the apricot mixture thickens and holds its shape on a spoon, stirring frequently to prevent sticking. Remove from heat.

❹ Ladle the hot mixture into a hot jar, leaving ½-inch headspace. Remove air bubbles. Wipe the jar rim. Center the lid on the jar. Apply the band, and adjust to fingertip-tight. Place the jar in the boiling water canner. Repeat until all the jars are filled.

❺ Process ½-pint and 1-pint jars 10 minutes, adjusting for altitude. Turn off heat; remove the lid, and let the jars stand 5 minutes. Remove the jars and cool.

PEAR BUTTER

**This versatile recipe is a wonderful way to get adventurous
with spices and seasonings. Add star anise, ginger, or a fruity red wine.**

6 pounds pears (18 to 24 medium),
   rinsed and peeled

¼ cup lemon juice

Liquid, Sweetener, and Seasoning,
   as desired from chart (page 124)

❶ Core and chop the pears. Bring the chopped pears and the lemon juice to a boil in a 6-quart stainless-steel or enameled Dutch oven; reduce heat, cover, and simmer until very soft. Remove from heat. Let cool slightly. Process, in batches, in a food mill, food processor, or blender until smooth.

❷ Return the pear mixture to the Dutch oven; stir in the desired liquid, sweetener, and seasoning, beginning with 1 cup sweetener. (If desired, gradually add more sweetener to taste, up to 2 cups.)

❸ Cook at a gentle boil over medium until the pear mixture thickens and holds its shape on a spoon, stirring frequently to prevent sticking. Remove from heat.

❹ Ladle the hot mixture into a hot jar, leaving ½-inch headspace. Remove air bubbles. Wipe the jar rim. Center the lid on the jar. Apply the band, and adjust to fingertip-tight. Place the jar in the boiling water canner. Repeat until all the jars are filled.

❺ Process ½-pint and 1-pint jars 10 minutes, adjusting for altitude. Turn off heat; remove the lid, and let the jars stand 5 minutes. Remove the jars and cool.

APPLE BUTTER

Apple butter is basically applesauce (page 134) cooked down until the apples caramelize. The resulting dark brown spread is often flavored using apple cider, cinnamon, allspice, and cloves. Using brown sugar instead of white will give it an even richer molasses flavor.

❶ Core and chop the apples. Bring the apples to a boil in a 6-quart stainless-steel or enameled Dutch oven; reduce heat, cover, and simmer until very soft. Remove from heat. Let cool slightly. Process, in batches, in a food mill, food processor or blender until smooth.

❷ Return the apple puree to the Dutch oven; stir in the desired liquid, sweetener, and seasoning, beginning with 1 cup sweetener. (If desired, gradually add more sweetener to taste, up to 2 cups.)

❸ Cook at a gentle boil over medium until the apple mixture thickens and holds its shape on a spoon, stirring frequently to prevent sticking. Remove from heat.

❹ Ladle the hot mixture into a hot jar, leaving ½-inch headspace. Remove air bubbles. Wipe the jar rim. Center the lid on the jar. Apply the band, and adjust to fingertip-tight. Place the jar in the boiling water canner. Repeat until all the jars are filled.

❺ Process ½-pint and 1-pint jars 10 minutes, adjusting for altitude. Turn off heat; remove the lid, and let the jars stand 5 minutes. Remove the jars and cool.

4 pounds apples (about 12 to 16 medium), rinsed and peeled

Liquid, Sweetener, and Seasoning, as desired from chart (page 124)

TIP

For a nice balanced flavor, choose a mix of apples, including Golden Delicious, McIntosh, or Granny Smith. Or use beautiful heirloom varieties such as Gala, Jonagold, or Cortland. You can leave the skins on to retain more color and taste.

FRUIT BUTTERS and SAUCES

BLUEBERRY BUTTER

MAKES ABOUT 6 (½-PINT) JARS

This smooth, fruity butter is wonderful stirred into morning oatmeal, slathered on toast, or dolloped on pancakes.

❶ Rinse the blueberries under cold running water; drain. Combine the blueberries and 2 cups water in an 8-quart stainless-steel or enameled Dutch oven; bring to a boil over medium-high, crushing berries with a potato masher. Reduce heat, and simmer 12 minutes, stirring occasionally.

❷ Pour the blueberry mixture through a mesh strainer lined with 3 layers of dampened cheesecloth into a bowl. Let drain 30 minutes or until the juice measures 2½ cups. (To avoid cloudy butter, do not press or squeeze the blueberry mixture.) Reserve the juice for another use. Process the blueberry mixture in a food processor 1 minute or until very smooth. Combine the blueberry mixture, sugar, and remaining ingredients in a 6-quart stainless-steel or enameled Dutch oven. Bring to a boil over medium, stirring often. Reduce heat, and simmer, stirring often, 1 hour or until the mixture thickens and holds its shape on a spoon.

❸ Ladle the hot blueberry butter into a hot jar, leaving ½-inch headspace. Remove air bubbles. Wipe the jar rim. Center the lid on the jar. Apply the band, and adjust to fingertip-tight. Place the jar in the boiling water canner. Repeat until all the jars are filled.

❹ Process the jars 10 minutes, adjusting for altitude. Turn off heat; remove the lid, and let the jars stand 5 minutes. Remove the jars and cool.

4½ pounds fresh blueberries

2 cups water

Cheesecloth

3 cups sugar

1 tablespoon lemon zest

1½ tablespoons lemon juice

¼ teaspoon ground nutmeg

CRANAPPLE BUTTER

This luscious spiced butter combines two popular fruit flavors. It is equally good as a topping for yogurt or a turkey sandwich.

6 pounds apples (about 18 to 24 medium)

2 quarts bottled cranberry juice cocktail (64 ounces)

4 cups sugar

2 teaspoons ground cinnamon

½ teaspoon ground nutmeg

❶ Rinse the apples under cold running water; drain. Core and peel the apples. Cut the apples lengthwise into eighths.

❷ Combine the apples and the cranberry juice cocktail in a large stainless-steel or enameled saucepan. Cook the apples at a simmer (180°F) until soft. Process the mixture, in batches, using a food mill, food processor, or blender until the mixture is smooth. Return the apple mixture to the saucepan. Add the sugar and the spices, stirring until the sugar dissolves. Cook at a gentle boil over medium until the apple mixture thickens and holds its shape on a spoon, stirring frequently to prevent sticking. Remove from heat.

❸ Ladle the hot mixture into a hot jar, leaving ½-inch headspace. Remove air bubbles. Wipe the jar rim. Center the lid on the jar. Apply the band, and adjust to fingertip-tight. Place the jar in the boiling water canner. Repeat until all the jars are filled.

❹ Process the jars 10 minutes, adjusting for altitude. Turn off heat; remove the lid, and let the jars stand 5 minutes. Remove the jars and cool.

HABANERO-CARROT BUTTER

MAKES ABOUT 5 (½-PINT) JARS

Fresh carrots take on a new flavor in this delicious sweet and spicy butter. Serve it as a garnish for tacos or stir it into guacamole or mayonnaise for a quick dipping sauce for wings, chips, or veggies.

① Bring all the ingredients, except the cilantro, to a boil in a 4-quart stainless-steel or enameled Dutch oven; reduce heat, cover, and simmer 30 minutes or until carrots are very soft. Remove from heat, and cool slightly, about 5 minutes.

② Process the carrot mixture and cilantro, in batches, in a blender or food processor until smooth, stopping to scrape down sides as needed.

③ Return the carrot mixture to the Dutch oven. Bring to a boil; reduce heat, and simmer, uncovered, 10 to 15 minutes or until the mixture thickens and holds its shape on a spoon.

④ Ladle the hot carrot mixture into a hot jar, leaving ½-inch headspace. Remove air bubbles. Wipe the jar rim. Center the lid on the jar. Apply the band, and adjust to fingertip-tight. Place the jar in the boiling water canner. Repeat until all the jars are filled.

⑤ Process the jars 10 minutes, adjusting for altitude. Turn off heat; remove the lid, and let the jars stand 5 minutes. Remove the jars and cool.

- 2 pounds carrots, peeled and sliced
- 1 cup water
- 1 cup white wine vinegar (5% acidity)
- ¾ cup finely chopped onion
- ½ cup bottled lime juice
- 1 teaspoon table salt
- 4 garlic cloves, chopped
- 3 habanero peppers, seeded and chopped
- ⅓ cup chopped fresh cilantro

APPLESAUCE

Using a mix of tart and sweet apple varieties will yield a balanced flavor. Choosing sweeter apples such as Fuji, Honeycrisp, and Gala allows you to reduce or omit additional sugar.

6 pounds apples, peeled, cored, and quartered

⅔ cup sugar

½ cup water

❶ Combine all the ingredients in a 6-quart stainless-steel or enameled Dutch oven. Cook over medium-low 25 minutes or until apples are very tender, stirring occasionally. Remove from heat. Let cool slightly.

❷ Process, in batches, in a food mill or food processor until smooth. Or crush the apple mixture with a potato masher for a chunkier applesauce.

❸ Ladle the hot applesauce into a hot jar, leaving ½-inch headspace. Remove air bubbles. Wipe the jar rim. Center the lid on the jar. Apply the band, and adjust to fingertip-tight. Place the jar in the boiling water canner. Repeat until all the jars are filled.

❹ Process the jars 20 minutes, adjusting for altitude. Turn off heat; remove the lid, and let the jars stand 5 minutes. Remove the jars and cool.

TIP

You may opt to leave the apples unpeeled for easier prep. Note that red-skinned apples will impart a rosy color to your sauce. If you prefer a creamy yellow color, peel the apples before cooking. (Use a mesh strainer to remove any solids.)

DIJON MUSTARD

MAKES ABOUT 6 (4-OUNCE) JARS

You'll find yourself using this pantry staple on everything. It is excellent in a vinaigrette, combined with brown sugar as a rub on ham, or as a spread on your favorite sandwiches.

2 cups chopped onion (about 3 medium)

2 cups Pinot Grigio or other dry white wine

1 cup white wine vinegar (5% acidity)

1 teaspoon table salt

6 garlic cloves, coarsely chopped

4 black peppercorns

1 rosemary sprig

1 cup yellow mustard seeds

⅓ cup dry mustard

2⅔ cups water

❶ Combine the first 7 ingredients in a large stainless-steel or enameled saucepan. Bring to a boil over high; reduce heat, and simmer, uncovered, 15 to 20 minutes or until the onion is very soft, stirring occasionally. Remove pan from heat; pour the onion mixture through a mesh strainer into a glass or stainless-steel bowl. Discard solids.

❷ Stir the mustard seeds and dry mustard into the onion mixture. Cover and let stand at room temperature at least 24 hours, but no longer than 48 hours.

❸ Process the mustard mixture in a blender or food processor, adding the water until consistency of cooked oatmeal.

❹ Transfer the mustard to a small stainless-steel or enameled saucepan. Bring to a boil, stirring often; reduce heat, and simmer, uncovered, 5 minutes.

❺ Ladle the hot mustard into a hot jar, leaving ½-inch headspace. Remove air bubbles. Wipe the jar rim. Center the lid on the jar. Apply the band, and adjust to fingertip-tight. Place the jar in the boiling water canner. Repeat until all the jars are filled.

❻ Process the jars 10 minutes, adjusting for altitude. Turn off heat; remove the lid, and let the jars stand 5 minutes. Remove the jars and cool.

KETCHUP

**Much tastier than store-bought, this ketchup is also
lower in sugar and salt than commercial brands.**

❶ Tie celery seeds, cloves, cinnamon sticks and allspice in a square of cheesecloth, creating a spice bag.

❷ Combine the vinegar and spice bag in a stainless-steel or enameled saucepan. Bring to a boil over high. Remove from heat and let stand 25 minutes. Discard spice bag.

❸ Combine tomatoes, onion, and cayenne in a clean large stainless-steel or enameled saucepan. Bring to a boil over high, stirring frequently. Reduce heat and boil gently 20 minutes. Add infused vinegar and boil gently until vegetables are soft and mixture begins to thicken, about 30 minutes.

❹ Transfer mixture, working in batches, to a mesh strainer placed over a glass or stainless-steel bowl and press with the back of a spoon to extract all the liquid. (This can also be done using a food mill.) Discard solids.

❺ Return the liquid to the saucepan. Add the sugar and salt. Bring to a boil over medium heat, stirring occasionally. Reduce heat and boil gently, stirring frequently, until volume is reduced by half and the mixture is almost the consistency of commercial ketchup, about 45 minutes.

❻ Ladle the hot ketchup into a hot jar, leaving ½-inch headspace. Remove air bubbles. Wipe the jar rim. Center the lid on the jar. Apply the band, and adjust to fingertip-tight. Place the jar in the boiling water canner. Repeat until all the jars are filled.

❼ Process the jars for 15 minutes, adjusting for altitude. Turn off heat; remove the lid, and let the jars stand 5 minutes. Remove the jars and cool.

3 tablespoons celery seeds

4 teaspoons whole cloves

2 cinnamon sticks, broken into pieces

1½ teaspoons whole allspice

Cheesecloth

3 cups apple cider vinegar

24 pounds tomatoes, cored and quartered (about 72 medium)

3 cups chopped onion (about 4 medium)

1 teaspoon cayenne pepper

1½ cups sugar

¼ cup Ball® Salt for Pickling & Preserving

CHERYL'S PERFECT BBQ SAUCE

MAKES ABOUT 5 (½-PINT) JARS

**This is a sweet and smoky BBQ sauce that makes
a great addition to any grilled meat.**

3 cups ketchup

⅓ cup water

6 tablespoons packed brown
sugar

6 tablespoons Worcestershire
sauce

1 tablespoon white vinegar
(5% acidity)

3 tablespoons honey

3 tablespoons molasses

2 teaspoons dry mustard

1 teaspoon table salt

1 teaspoon garlic powder

1 teaspoon chili powder

1 teaspoon smoked paprika

1 teaspoon freshly ground black
pepper

❶ Combine all the ingredients in a medium stainless-steel or enameled saucepan. Cook over medium-low 15 minutes, stirring occasionally.

❷ Ladle the hot sauce into a hot jar, leaving ½-inch headspace. Remove air bubbles. Wipe the jar rim. Center the lid on the jar. Apply the band, and adjust to fingertip-tight. Place the jar in the boiling water canner. Repeat until all the jars are filled.

❸ Process the jars 10 minutes, adjusting for altitude. Turn off heat; remove the lid, and let the jars stand 5 minutes. Remove the jars and cool.

CRANBERRY SAUCE

MAKES ABOUT 4 (½-PINT) JARS OR 2 (1-PINT) JARS

A classic Thanksgiving staple with turkey and dressing, this is just as great anytime of the year served with Monte Cristo sandwiches or Swedish pancakes.

❶ Rinse the cranberries under cold running water; drain. Discard any crushed or bruised cranberries.

❷ Combine the cranberries and the water in a large stainless-steel or enameled saucepan. Boil over medium-high until skins begin to split. Puree the mixture using a food mill or food strainer to remove peels and seeds; discard solids. Return the mixture to the large saucepan. Add the sugar to the cranberry mixture, and cook over medium-high, stirring until the sugar dissolves. Boil the mixture almost to the gelling point (220°F).

❸ Ladle the hot cranberry sauce into a hot jar, leaving ½-inch headspace. Remove air bubbles. Wipe the jar rim. Center the lid on the jar. Apply the band, and adjust to fingertip-tight. Place the jar in the boiling water canner. Repeat until all the jars are filled.

❹ Process the jars 15 minutes, adjusting for altitude. Turn off heat; remove the lid, and let the jars stand 5 minutes. Remove the jars and cool.

4½ cups fresh cranberries (about 1½ pounds)

1¾ cups water

2 cups sugar

5

....

TOMATOES

Preserving a summer's bounty of fresh, ripe tomatoes keeps your pantry full year-round. Any variety of tomato is good for canning—just be sure to pick fresh, fully ripe tomatoes free of bruises or cracks for the best color and flavor. Due to the varying levels of acid found in tomatoes, they are on the borderline of proper pH levels, so they need extra attention to ensure they are safe for water bath canning. For this reason, we've added Ball® Citric Acid or lemon juice to ensure a safe and successful preserving experience.

HOW TO CAN TOMATOES

You will need:

- Tested recipe and ingredients
- Glass preserving jars with lids and bands (always start with new lids)
- Water bath canner or a large, deep stockpot with lid and rack
- Jar lifter
- Common kitchen utensils, including measuring cups and spoons, large ladle, kitchen towel, and rubber spatula
- Large stainless-steel or enameled saucepan or Dutch oven
- Canning funnel
- Bubble remover and headspace measuring tool
- Labels

TIPS

Choose ripe tomatoes that are bruise- and blemish-free. Cut away any cracked portions.

You may also use a dishwasher to wash and heat the jars.

STEP 1: HEAT JARS Examine the jars for defects. Place a canning rack at the bottom of the canner and fill halfway with water. Place the jars in and bring the water almost to a simmer over medium. **IMPORTANT:** Keep the jars hot until ready to fill to prevent jar breakage. Wash the lids and bands in warm soapy water, rinse, and set aside.

STEP 2: PREP INGREDIENTS Rinse the tomatoes under cold running water; drain. Cut a small "x" in the blossom end of each tomato with a paring knife. Dip in boiling water 30 to 60 seconds; immediately plunge into cold water. Core and peel. Halve, quarter, or leave whole, as desired.

RAW PACK

STEP 3: COOK Raw Pack is the faster prep method. Bring 2 cups water to a boil; reduce heat to a simmer. Keep water hot.

STEP 4: FILL Working with one hot jar at a time, add citric acid or bottled lemon juice (to ensure a safe pH) and salt (optional).

Pack the raw peeled tomatoes into the hot jar, leaving ½-inch headspace. Ladle hot water over the tomatoes, leaving ½-inch headspace. Remove air bubbles. Wipe the rim and top of the jar with a clean, damp towel. Center the lid onto the jar; apply the band, and adjust until fingertip-tight.

HOT PACK

STEP 3: COOK Hot Pack requires cooking the tomatoes before they go into the jars. Bring the tomatoes and just enough water to cover to a boil over medium-high in a large stainless-steel or enameled Dutch oven; reduce heat, and simmer 5 minutes.

STEP 4: FILL Working with one hot jar at a time, add the citric acid or bottled lemon juice and salt (optional). Pack the hot tomatoes into the hot jar, with a slotted spoon, leaving ½-inch headspace.

Ladle the hot cooking liquid over the tomatoes, leaving ½-inch headspace. Remove air bubbles. Wipe the rim and top of the jar with a damp towel to remove any food residue. Center the lid onto the jar; apply the band, and adjust until fingertip-tight.

STEP 5: PROCESS Place the filled jar in the canner. Repeat one at a time until all the jars are filled. Make sure the water covers the jars. Place the lid on and bring the water to a full rolling boil. Once the water is boiling, set the timer for 40 minutes for pint jars; for 45 minutes for quart jars, adjusting for altitude, (page 16). Turn off the heat and remove the lid. Let the canner cool 5 minutes before removing the jars.

STEP 6: Using the jar lifter, remove the jars from the canner and set upright on a towel or cutting board, leaving at least 2 inches beween the jars. Leave undisturbed for at least 12 hours. The bands may loosen during processing but should not be retightened, as this may interfere with the sealing process.

STEP 7: TEST & STORE Check the lids for vacuum seals after stand time. The lids should not flex up and down when the center is pressed. Remove the bands. Gently try to lift off the lid with your fingertips. If the lid cannot be lifted off, the lid has a good seal. Wipe the jars and lids with a clean, damp cloth. Label and store in a cool, dry, dark place up to 1 year.

TOMATOES

WHOLE, HALVED, of QUARTERED TOMATOES

MAKES ABOUT 2 (1-PINT) JARS OR 1 (1-QUART) JAR

Choose the best-quality tomatoes to preserve. Look for plump, ripe fruit with unblemished skin.

2½ to 3½ pounds ripe tomatoes (about 8 to 10 medium)

Water

½ teaspoon Ball® Citric Acid or 2 tablespoons bottled lemon juice to each hot quart jar or ¼ teaspoon Ball® Citric Acid or 1 tablespoon bottled lemon juice to each hot pint jar

1 teaspoon table salt (optional)

❶ Rinse the tomatoes under cold running water; drain. Cut an "x" in the blossom end of the tomato with a paring knife. Dip in boiling water 30 to 60 seconds. Immediately dip in cold water. Slip off the skins. Core and peel. Halve, quarter, or leave whole, as desired.

❷ Choose a packing method.

RAW PACK: Bring about 2 to 4 cups water to boil in a saucepan; reduce heat to a simmer. Keep water hot.

HOT PACK: Place the peeled tomatoes into a large saucepan. Add just enough water to cover. Bring to a boil over medium-high. Boil genty 5 minutes, stirring to prevent sticking.

❸ Working with one hot jar at a time, add ½ teaspoon Ball® Citric Acid or 2 tablespoons bottled lemon juice to each hot quart jar. Add ¼ teaspoon Ball® Citric Acid or 1 tablespoon bottled lemon juice to each hot pint jar. Add salt, if desired, ½ teaspoon for each pint jar or 1 teaspoon for each quart.

RAW PACK: Pack the raw peeled tomatoes into the hot jar, leaving ½-inch headspace. Ladle hot water over tomatoes, leaving ½-inch headspace.

HOT PACK: Pack the cooked tomatoes into the hot jar, leaving ½-inch headspace. Ladle hot cooking liquid over tomatoes, leaving ½-inch headspace.

❹ Remove air bubbles. Wipe the jar rim. Center the lid on the jar. Apply the band, and adjust to fingertip-tight. Place the jar in the boiling water canner. Repeat until all the jars are filled.

❺ Process the jars 40 minutes for pints, or 45 minutes for quarts, adjusting for altitude. Turn off heat; remove the lid, and let the jars stand 5 minutes. Remove the jars and cool.

CRUSHED TOMATOES

MAKES ABOUT 2 (1-PINT) JARS OR 1 (1-QUART) JAR

Crushed tomatoes resemble whole or halved tomatoes in flavor, but since they are crushed they're ideal for sauce, soup, and stew recipes.

❶ Rinse the tomatoes under cold running water; drain. Cut an "x" in the blossom end of the tomato with a paring knife. Dip in boiling water 30 to 60 seconds. Immediately dip in cold water. Slip off skins. Trim away any green areas and cut out core. Cut the tomatoes into quarters to measure about 2 cups.

❷ Transfer to a large stainless-steel or enameled saucepan and bring to a boil over medium-high. Using a potato masher, crush the tomatoes to release the juices. While maintaining a gentle boil and stirring to prevent scorching, quarter additional tomatoes and add to the saucepan as you work. The remaining tomatoes do not need to be crushed, as they will soften with heating and stirring. Continue until all the tomatoes are added, and then boil gently 5 minutes.

❸ Add ½ teaspoon Ball® Citric Acid or 2 tablespoons bottled lemon juice to each hot quart jar. Add ¼ teaspoon Ball® Citric Acid or 1 tablespoon bottled lemon juice to each hot pint jar.

❹ Pack the hot tomatoes into the hot jars, leaving ½-inch headspace. Press the tomatoes into the jar until the spaces between them fill with juice, leaving ½-inch headspace. Add 1 teaspoon salt to each quart jar or ½ teaspoon to each pint jar, if desired. Remove air bubbles. Wipe the jar rim. Center the lid on the jar. Apply the band, and adjust to fingertip-tight. Place the jar in the boiling water canner. Repeat until all the jars are filled.

❺ Process the jars for 35 minutes for pints, or 45 minutes for quarts, adjusting for altitude. Turn off heat; remove the lid, and let the jars stand 5 minutes. Remove the jars and cool.

2¾ pounds ripe tomatoes (about 8 medium)

½ teaspoon Ball® Citric Acid or 2 tablespoons bottled lemon juice to each hot quart jar or ¼ teaspoon Ball® Citric Acid or 1 tablespoon bottled lemon juice to each hot pint jar

Salt (optional) 1 teaspoon table salt to each quart jar or ½ teaspoon table salt to each pint jar, if desired

ROASTED ROMA TOMATOES

**Roasting tomatoes brings out a sweet smokiness that
adds an extra flavor dimension.**

12 pounds ripe plum tomatoes
(about 60 medium)

4 garlic heads

¼ cup extra-virgin olive oil

1½ cups chopped onion

1 tablespoon minced fresh
oregano

1 teaspoon table salt

½ teaspoon coarsely ground black
pepper

Ball® Citric Acid or bottled lemon
juice

❶ Rinse the tomatoes under cold running water; drain.

❷ Roast the tomatoes on a grill or under a broiler until the skins
begin to wrinkle and become lightly blackened in spots, turning
to roast evenly on all sides. Remove from heat. Place the roasted
tomatoes in a paper bag and close. Cool until the tomatoes are easy
to handle, about 15 minutes. Peel and core the tomatoes. Cut the
tomatoes in half crosswise and remove the seeds. Cut the tomatoes
into ½-inch chunks; set aside. Place the garlic on aluminum foil and
drizzle the olive oil over the garlic. Wrap the foil around the garlic,
sealing the edges tightly. Roast the garlic at 350°F until tender, about
30 minutes. Cool until the garlic is easy to handle. Separate the
garlic cloves and peel. Combine the tomatoes, garlic, onion, and
next 3 ingredients in a large stainless-steel or enameled saucepan.
Cook over medium until hot, about 30 minutes.

❸ Add ¼ teaspoon citric acid or 1 tablespoon bottled lemon juice
to a hot pint jar; ½ teaspoon citric acid or 2 tablespoons bottle
lemon juice to a hot quart jar. Pack the tomato mixture into a jar,
leaving ½-inch headspace. Remove air bubbles. Wipe the jar rim.
Center the lid on the jar. Apply the band, and adjust to fingertip-
tight. Place the jar in the boiling water canner. Repeat until all the
jars are filled.

❹ Process the jars for 1 hour and 25 minutes, adjusting for altitude.
Turn off heat; remove the lid, and let the jars stand 5 minutes.
Remove the jars and cool.

TOMATO PASTE

The concentrated flavor of tomato paste can add a big boost to many recipes. The size and meatiness of plum tomatoes makes them favorites for canning.

16 pounds ripe plum tomatoes (about 48 medium)

1½ cups chopped red bell pepper

1 teaspoon table salt (optional)

2 bay leaves

1 garlic clove (optional)

Ball® Citric Acid or bottled lemon juice

① Rinse the tomatoes under cold running water; drain. Combine the tomatoes, bell pepper, and salt, if desired, in a large stainless-steel or enameled saucepan. Cook over medium 1 hour, stirring to prevent sticking. Process the tomato mixture using a food mill to remove peels and seeds until smooth. Return the puree to the saucepan. Add the bay leaves and, if desired, the garlic. Cook over medium, stirring frequently, until the mixture is thick enough to mound on a spoon, about 2½ hours. Remove and discard the bay leaves and the garlic.

② Add ¼ teaspoon citric acid or 1½ teaspoons bottled lemon juice to a hot jar. Ladle the hot paste into the jar, leaving ½-inch headspace. Remove air bubbles. Wipe the jar rim. Center the lid on the jar. Apply the band, and adjust to fingertip-tight. Place the jar in the boiling water canner. Repeat until all the jars are filled.

③ Process the jars for 45 minutes, adjusting for altitude. Turn off heat; remove the lid, and let the jars stand 5 minutes. Remove the jars and cool.

BASIL-GARLIC TOMATO SAUCE

**With herbs and aromatics already cooked in, this
sauce is a real time-saving pantry staple.**

① Rinse the tomatoes under cold running water; drain. Remove the core and the blossom end from the tomatoes. Cut the tomatoes into quarters.

② Sauté the onion and the garlic in the olive oil in a large stainless-steel or enameled saucepan until the onion is tender. Add the tomatoes and simmer 20 minutes, stirring occasionally. Process the tomato mixture using a food mill or food processor until smooth. Stir in the basil. Cook the tomato mixture, uncovered, over medium-high until reduced by half, stirring to prevent sticking.

③ Add ¼ teaspoon citric acid or 1 tablespoon bottled lemon juice to a hot pint jar. Add ½ teaspoon citric acid or 2 tablespoons bottled lemon juice to a hot quart jar. Pack the tomato mixture into a jar, leaving ½-inch headspace. Remove air bubbles. Wipe the jar rim. Center the lid on the jar. Apply the band, and adjust to fingertip-tight. Place the jar in the boiling water canner. Repeat until all the jars are filled.

④ Process the jars for 35 minutes for pint jars, or 40 minutes for quart jars, adjusting for altitude. Turn off heat; remove the lid, and let the jars stand 5 minutes. Remove the jars and cool.

20 pounds ripe tomatoes (about 60 medium)

1 cup chopped onion

8 garlic cloves, minced

1 tablespoon extra-virgin olive oil

¼ cup finely minced fresh basil

Ball® Citric Acid or bottled lemon juice

TOMATOES

TOMATO SAUCE

You can use this basic tomato sauce unseasoned as a base for your recipes or simmer in one of the Seasoning Blends to add flair to your meals.

15 pounds ripe plum tomatoes (about 75 medium)

Choice of seasoning blend (optional) (below)

1½ teaspoons Ball® Citric Acid or ⅓ cup bottled lemon juice

1 tablespoon table salt (optional)

❶ Rinse the tomatoes under cold running water; drain. Remove the core and the blossom end from the tomatoes. Cut the tomatoes into quarters. Bring the tomatoes to a boil in a large stainless-steel or enameled stockpot; reduce heat, and simmer, uncovered, 15 minutes, stirring occasionally. Press the tomato mixture, in batches, through a food mill, into a large bowl; discard skins and seeds. Return each batch of the tomato puree to the stockpot. Add the seasoning blend, if desired. Bring to a boil; reduce heat, and simmer 45 minutes or until reduced by half. Stir in the citric acid, and, if desired, salt.

❷ Ladle the hot tomato sauce into a hot jar, leaving ½-inch headspace. Remove air bubbles. Wipe the jar rim. Center the lid on the jar. Apply the band, and adjust to fingertip-tight. Place the jar in the boiling water canner. Repeat until all the jars are filled.

❸ Process the pint jars 35 minutes or 40 minutes for quart jars, adjusting for altitude. Turn off heat; remove the lid, and let the jars stand 5 minutes. Remove the jars and cool.

CHANGE IT UP

Italian Seasoning Blend 2 tablespoons dried oregano, 2 tablespoons dried basil, 1 tablespoon garlic powder, 2 teaspoons dried thyme, 2 teaspoons crushed red pepper (optional). Combine all the ingredients in a small bowl. Makes about 6 tablespoons

Creole Seasoning Blend 1 tablespoon sweet paprika, 1 tablespoon hot paprika, 1 tablespoon cayenne pepper, 1 tablespoon dried oregano, 2 teaspoons garlic powder, 2 teaspoons onion powder, 2 teaspoons freshly ground black pepper, 2 teaspoons dried thyme, 1 teaspoon celery seeds, 1 teaspoon ground white pepper. Combine all the ingredients in a small bowl. Makes about ½ cup

TOMATO JUICE

The possibilites are endless with this basic recipe. Not only will it enhance drinks, it can also be used as a terrific base for vegetable or minestrone soups. The beet kicks up the color without affecting the flavor.

1 Rinse the tomatoes under cold running water; drain. Core the tomatoes and cut into quarters. Bring the tomatoes, any accumulated juices, and the diced beet to a boil in a large stainless-steel or enameled stockpot, stirring often; reduce heat, and simmer, uncovered, 15 minutes or until the vegetables are very tender, stirring often.

2 Press the tomato mixture, in batches, through a food mill, into a large bowl; discard the skins and seeds. Return the tomato juice to the stockpot. Cook over medium, stirring often, until a thermometer registers 190°F; remove from heat. Stir in the salt and the citric acid or lemon juice. Cook over medium heat, stirring often, until a thermometer registers 190°F; remove from heat.

3 Ladle the hot juice into a hot jar, leaving ½-inch headspace. Remove air bubbles. Wipe the jar rim. Center the lid on the jar. Apply the band, and adjust to fingertip-tight. Place the jar in the boiling water canner. Repeat until all the jars are filled.

4 Process the jars 40 minutes, adjusting for altitude. Turn off heat; remove the lid, and let the jars stand 5 minutes. Remove the jars and cool.

14 pounds ripe tomatoes (about 70 medium)

1 large red beet, peeled and cut into ¼-inch cubes

1 tablespoon table salt or celery salt

2 teaspoons Ball® Citric Acid or ½ cup bottled lemon juice

SAUCY SLOPPY JOE STARTER

MAKES ABOUT 4 (1-PINT) JARS

**Grab a jar of your own homemade sauce to make
quick work of this popular sandwich filling.**

3 cups finely chopped green bell
pepper (about 2 large)

3 cups finely chopped red bell
pepper (about 2 large)

2 cups diced onion (about 2 large)

4 teaspoons table salt

2 teaspoons freshly ground black
pepper

½ cup Tomato Paste (page 150) or
1 (6-ounce) can store-bought
tomato paste

4 cups Tomato Sauce (page 152)

½ cup apple cider vinegar
(5% acidity)

½ cup Dijon mustard

¼ cup packed brown sugar

1 Line a large rimmed baking sheet with aluminum foil; coat foil with cooking spray. Spread the bell peppers and onions on the prepared pan in an even layer. Stir in the salt and the pepper. Bake at 375°F for 20 minutes or until the vegetables are very tender and beginning to brown, stirring occasionally.

2 Transfer the onion mixture to a large skillet. Stir in the Tomato Paste; cook, uncovered, stirring often, 5 minutes until the mixture begins to thicken. Stir in the Tomato Sauce and remaining ingredients. Bring to a boil; reduce heat, and simmer, uncovered, stirring often, 5 minutes or until the sauce is slightly thickened.

3 Ladle the hot sauce into a hot jar, leaving ½-inch headspace. Remove air bubbles. Wipe the jar rim. Center the lid on the jar. Apply the band, and adjust to fingertip-tight. Place the jar in the boiling water canner. Repeat until all the jars are filled.

4 Process the jars 20 minutes, adjusting for altitude. Turn off heat; remove the lid, and let the jars stand 5 minutes. Remove the jars and cool.

CORN 𝑎𝑛𝑑 CHERRY TOMATO SALSA

MAKES ABOUT 6 (½-PINT) JARS

This tasty salsa will remind you of summer even when there's frost on the window panes.

❶ Bring all the ingredients to a boil in a large stainless-steel or enameled saucepan. Reduce heat and simmer 5 minutes, stirring occasionally.

❷ Ladle the hot salsa into a hot jar, leaving ½-inch headspace. Remove air bubbles. Wipe the jar rim. Center the lid on the jar. Apply the band, and adjust to fingertip-tight. Place the jar in the boiling water canner. Repeat until all the jars are filled.

❸ Process the jars 15 minutes, adjusting for altitude. Turn off heat; remove the lid, and let the jars stand 5 minutes. Remove the jars and cool.

NOTE: The use of fresh lime juice in this recipe is for the purpose of fresh flavor and has been verified as safe by scientific testing.

1¾ pounds cherry tomatoes, quartered

1 cup fresh corn kernels (about 2 large ears)

½ cup finely chopped red onion

¼ cup fresh lime juice (about 3 limes)

3 tablespoons chopped fresh cilantro

1 teaspoon table salt

1 to 2 jalapeño peppers, seeded and minced

TOMATO-JALAPEÑO SALSA

MAKES ABOUT 6 (½-PINT) JARS

**This is a great basic tomato salsa to keep on hand.
Garnish with fresh cilantro when serving.**

2 pounds ripe plum tomatoes, chopped (about 10 medium)

1 medium onion, finely chopped

½ cup fresh lime juice (about 6 limes)

¼ cup chopped fresh cilantro

1 teaspoon table salt

½ teaspoon freshly ground black pepper

2 garlic cloves, minced

2 jalapeño peppers, seeded and minced

❶ Bring all the ingredients to a boil in a large stainless-steel or enameled saucepan; reduce heat, and simmer 5 minutes, stirring occasionally.

❷ Ladle the hot salsa into a hot jar, leaving ½-inch headspace. Remove air bubbles. Wipe the jar rim. Center the lid on the jar. Apply the band, and adjust to fingertip-tight. Place the jar in the boiling water canner. Repeat until all the jars are filled.

❸ Process the jars 15 minutes, adjusting for altitude. Turn off heat; remove the lid, and let the jars stand 5 minutes. Remove the jars and cool.

NOTE: The use of fresh lime juice in this recipe is for the purpose of fresh flavor and has been verified as safe by scientific testing.

HABANERO-TOMATILLO SALSA

MAKES ABOUT 6 (½-PINT) JARS

**Habanero peppers are among the hottest chiles. This salsa
is brimming with flavor from the roasted tomatillos.**

❶ Line a large rimmed baking sheet with aluminum foil. Coat the foil with cooking spray. Arrange the tomatillos, stem side down, and onion, skin side down, on the prepared pan. Bake at 425°F for 20 minutes or until the tomatillos and onion are beginning to char and soften.

❷ Chop the tomatillos and place in a large stainless-steel or enameled saucepan. Peel the onion; chop the onion and add to the pan. Stir in the lime juice and remaining 3 ingredients. Bring to a boil; reduce heat, and simmer 5 minutes, stirring occasionally.

❸ Ladle the hot salsa into a hot jar, leaving ½-inch headspace. Remove air bubbles. Wipe the jar rim. Center the lid on the jar. Apply the band, and adjust to fingertip-tight. Place the jar in the boiling water canner. Repeat until all the jars are filled.

❹ Process the jars 15 minutes, adjusting for altitude. Turn off heat; remove the lid, and let the jars stand 5 minutes. Remove the jars and cool.

NOTE: The use of fresh lime juice in this recipe is for the purpose of fresh flavor and has been verified as safe by scientific testing.

2½ pounds tomatillos, husks removed (about 13 tomatillos)

1 red onion, quartered

¼ cup fresh lime juice (about 3 limes)

3 tablespoons chopped fresh cilantro

1 teaspoon table salt

4 habanero chile peppers, seeded and minced

GREEN TOMATO SALSA VERDE

MAKES ABOUT 6 (½-PINT) JARS

**Use this straight up as a sauce for enchiladas, or stir it into
a cheese dip or your morning breakfast burrito filling.**

2 pounds green tomatoes, finely chopped (about 6 tomatoes), or the same amount of tomatillos, husks removed and cleaned

1 cup finely chopped onion

1 teaspoon table salt

2 garlic cloves, minced

1 to 2 jalapeño or serrano peppers, seeded and finely chopped

½ cup chopped fresh cilantro

⅓ cup fresh lime juice (about 4 limes)

❶ Bring the first 5 ingredients to a boil in a large stainless-steel or enameled saucepan. Reduce heat and simmer 5 minutes, stirring occasionally. Stir in the cilantro and the lime juice.

❷ Ladle the hot salsa into a hot jar, leaving ½-inch headspace. Remove air bubbles. Wipe the jar rim. Center the lid on the jar. Apply the band, and adjust to fingertip-tight. Place the jar in the boiling water canner. Repeat until all the jars are filled.

❸ Process the jars 15 minutes, adjusting for altitude. Turn off heat; remove the lid, and let the jars stand 5 minutes. Remove the jars and cool.

NOTE: The use of fresh lime juice in this recipe is for the purpose of fresh flavor and has been verified as safe by scientific testing.

TOMATO-APPLE CHUTNEY

MAKES ABOUT 6 (1-PINT) JARS

**This spiced chutney is as good on top of crackers as it is
as an accompaniment with your favorite curry dishes.**

10 cups peeled, cored, and
    chopped tomatoes (about
    11 medium)

4 cups chopped apples
    (about 4 medium)

3 cups packed brown sugar

2 cups chopped cucumber

1½ cups chopped onion

1½ cups chopped red bell pepper

1 hot red chile pepper

1 cup dark raisins

1 garlic clove

1 tablespoon ground ginger

1 teaspoon Ball® Salt for Pickling
    & Preserving

1 teaspoon ground cinnamon

3 cups white vinegar (5% acidity)

❶ Combine all the ingredients in a large stainless-steel or enameled saucepan. Bring the mixture to a boil. Reduce heat to a simmer; simmer until the mixture begins to thicken, stirring to prevent sticking.

❷ Pack the hot chutney into a hot jar, leaving ½-inch headspace. Remove air bubbles. Wipe the jar rim. Center the lid on the jar. Apply the band, and adjust to fingertip-tight. Place the jar in the boiling water canner. Repeat until all the jars are filled.

❸ Process the jars 15 minutes, adjusting for altitude. Turn off heat; remove the lid, and let the jars stand 5 minutes. Remove the jars and cool.

THAI GREEN TOMATO CHUTNEY

This end-of-summer chutney combines late-season green tomatoes
with sweet ripe plums and has all the tangy, spicy notes of Thai cuisine.
Serve it as a condiment with grilled eggplant.

❶ Bring the first 7 ingredients to a boil in a 6-quart stainless-steel or enameled Dutch oven; reduce heat, and simmer, uncovered, 20 minutes or until the fruit begins to soften. Add the chile peppers and salt; simmer, stirring constantly, 25 minutes or until very thick. Stir in the cilantro. Remove from heat.

❷ Ladle the hot chutney into a hot jar, leaving ½-inch headspace. Remove air bubbles. Wipe the jar rim. Center the lid on the jar. Apply the band, and adjust to fingertip-tight. Place the jar in the boiling water canner. Repeat until all the jars are filled.

❸ Process the jars 15 minutes, adjusting for altitude. Turn off heat; remove the lid, and let the jars stand 5 minutes. Remove the jars and cool.

CHANGE IT UP

½ to 1 teaspoon cayenne pepper may be substituted for the Thai chile peppers.

Other varieties of plums, such as Italian prune plums, pluots, and green damson plums work nicely in this recipe, too.

2 pounds ripe red plums, pitted and coarsely chopped (about 7 medium)

1½ pounds green tomatoes, cored and coarsely chopped (about 5 medium)

1⅓ cups diced onion

¾ cup packed light brown sugar

½ cup rice vinegar

¼ cup lemon juice (about 2 large)

2 garlic cloves, minced

2 Thai chile peppers, seeded and minced

1 teaspoon table salt

¼ cup chopped fresh cilantro

6

PICKLES

Pickles, with their crunch and tartness, transform simply prepared meals into culinary adventures. Because of their versatility, pickles are the perfect condiments to have at your fingertips. The recipes featured here are made using the brined or fresh-pack method. You can choose to preserve your pickles in a water bath for longer term storage, or in some cases, you can refrigerate the pickles to enjoy almost immediately.

HOW TO FRESH-PACK PICKLES

You will need:

- Tested recipe and ingredients
- Glass preserving jars with lids and bands (always start with new lids)
- Water bath canner or a large, deep stockpot with lid and rack
- Jar lifter
- Common kitchen utensils, including measuring cups and spoons, large ladle, kitchen towel, and rubber spatula
- Large stainless-steel or enameled saucepan or Dutch oven
- Bubble remover and headspace measuring tool
- Labels

TIPS

Use only canning salt. Do not substitute with iodized, flake, rock, kosher, or sea salt, which will not measure the same.

Use high-grade apple cider vinegar or white distilled vinegar of 5% acidity. Do not change the amount of vinegar or increase the amount of water.

You may also use a dishwasher to wash and heat the jars.

Fresh-pack pickles can be eaten immediately but develop much better flavor if allowed to stand for a few weeks in the pantry.

STEP 1: PREP INGREDIENTS Prepare the vegetables according to the recipe. Rinse the vegetables under cold running water; drain. Trim the ends, if noted, and cut according to the recipe, making sure the vegetables are not more than 5 inches long so they'll fit in the jar.

If the recipe requires, place the vegetables in a large, clean container (such as a 12-quart food-safe plastic pail or basin). Dissolve pickling salt in water, and pour over the vegetables to help release extra liquid; cover and let stand overnight or as directed in the recipe. Drain.

STEP 2: HEAT JARS Examine the jars for defects. Place a canning rack at the bottom of the canner and fill halfway with water. Place the jars in and bring the water almost to a simmer over medium. **IMPORTANT:** Keep the jars hot until ready to fill to prevent jar breakage due to thermal shock. Wash the lids and bands in warm soapy water, rinse, and set aside.

STEP 3: COOK Make the brine. Combine the water, vinegar, sugar, spices, and pickling salt in a stainless-steel or enameled saucepan or Dutch oven. Bring to a boil, stirring until the salt dissolves.

STEP 4: FILL Working with 1 hot jar at a time, pack the vegetables into the jar, leaving ½-inch headspace. Ladle the hot pickling liquid over the vegetables, leaving ½-inch headspace. Add ⅛ teaspoon Ball® Pickle Crisp® Granules to the jar, if desired.

Remove air bubbles by sliding a bubble remover between the jar and food to release trapped air. Repeat around jar 2 or 3 times. Wipe the rim and top of the jar with a clean, damp cloth to remove any food residue, which can prevent a vacuum seal. Center the lid on the jar. Apply the band, and adjust to fingertip-tight. Repeat until all the jars are filled.

STEP 5: PROCESS Place the filled jar in canner. Make sure the water covers the jars by 1 inch. Place the lid on and bring the water to a full boil. Start timing for the length of time stated in the recipe (adjusting for altitude). Maintain a rolling boil throughout the processing period. After processing time is complete, turn off heat and remove the lid. Let the canner cool 5 minutes before removing the jars.

STEP 6: Using the jar lifter, remove the jars from the canner to cool and set upright on a towel or cutting bord, leaving at least 2 inches between jars. Leave the jars undisturbed for 12 to 24 hours. Bands should not be retightened, as this may interfere with the sealing process.

STEP 7: TEST & STORE Check the lids for vacuum seals after stand time. Lids should not flex up and down when center is pressed. Remove the bands. Gently try to lift off the lid with your fingertips. If the lid cannot be lifted off, the lid has a good seal. Wipe the jars and lids with a clean, damp cloth. Label and store in a cool, dry, dark place up to 1 year.

DILL PICKLE SPEARS

MAKES ABOUT 6 (1-PINT) JARS

This traditional pickle is a great recipe to start with if you're new to cucumber pickles. Brining the cucumbers before pickling helps keep them crunchy, and a pinch of Ball® Pickle Crisp® Granules ensures it.

1 Rinse the cucumbers under cold running water, and trim any that are longer than 5 inches so that they'll fit comfortably in the jar. Cut each cucumber lengthwise into quarters. Place the spears in a large, clean container (such as a 12- to 18-quart food-safe plastic pail or basin). Combine 1 gallon of the water and 6 tablespoons of the salt in a large pitcher, stirring until the salt dissolves. Pour over the cucumbers; cover and let stand at room temperature 24 hours. Drain; rinse under cold running water, and drain.

2 Combine remaining 1 quart water, vinegar, next 2 ingredients, and remaining ¼ cup salt in a stainless-steel or enameled saucepan. Bring to a boil, stirring until the salt and sugar dissolve.

3 Place 2 of the dill sprigs and 1 teaspoon of the mustard seeds into a hot jar, and pack tightly with the cucumber spears. Ladle the hot pickling liquid over the spears, leaving ½-inch headspace. Add ⅛ teaspoon Ball® Pickle Crisp® Granules to jar, if desired. Remove air bubbles. Wipe the jar rim. Center the lid on the jar. Apply the band, and adjust to fingertip-tight. Place the jar in the boiling water canner. Repeat until all the jars are filled.

4 Process the jars 10 minutes, adjusting for altitude. Turn off heat; remove the lid, and let the jars stand 5 minutes. Remove the jars and cool.

4 pounds (3- to 5-inch) pickling cucumbers

1 gallon plus 1 quart water

10 tablespoons Ball® Salt for Pickling and Preserving

3 cups white vinegar (5% acidity)

2 tablespoons sugar

1 tablespoon pickling spice

12 dill sprigs

2 tablespoons mustard seeds

Ball® Pickle Crisp® Granules (optional)

BREAD and BUTTER PICKLES

**This classic sweet-tart pickle is a staple in relish trays
and on burgers and sandwiches.**

4 pounds (4- to 6-inch) cucumbers

2 pounds onions, thinly sliced

⅓ cup Ball® Salt for Pickling &
  Preserving

2 cups sugar

2 tablespoons mustard seeds

2 teaspoons ground turmeric

2 teaspoons celery seeds

1 teaspoon ground ginger

1 teaspoon whole black
  peppercorns

3 cups white vinegar (5% acidity)

Ball® Pickle Crisp® Granules
  (optional)

❶ Rinse the cucumbers under cold running water; drain. Remove stem and 1/16 inch from blossom end of cucumbers. Cut the cucumbers crosswise into ¼-inch slices. Put the cucumbers and onions in a large bowl, layering with the salt. Cover with ice cubes. Let stand 1½ hours. Drain the cucumbers and onions. Rinse the cucumbers and onions under cold running water; drain.

❷ Combine the sugar, spices, and vinegar in a large stainless-steel or enameled saucepan. Bring the mixture to a boil, stirring until the sugar dissolves. Add the cucumbers and onions. Bring the mixture to a boil, stirring until the salt and sugar dissolve.

❸ Pack the hot pickles and liquid into a hot jar, leaving ½-inch headspace. Add ⅛ teaspoon Ball® Pickle Crisp® Granules to pint jar, if desired. Remove air bubbles. Wipe the jar rim. Center the lid on the jar. Apply the band, and adjust to fingertip-tight. Place the jar in the boiling water canner. Repeat until all the jars are filled.

❹ Process the jars 10 minutes, adjusting for altitude. Turn off heat; remove the lid, and let the jars stand 5 minutes. Remove the jars and cool.

TIP

Pickling cucumbers are small, crisp, unwaxed, and needn't be peeled. Wide mouth jars aren't essential for pickles, but they do make for easier packing.

PICKLED ASPARAGUS

MAKES ABOUT 6 (½-PINT) JARS

**Enjoy this spring vegetable year-round. Choose fresh
medium-thick spears and mix up the colors for a pretty jar.**

5 cups white vinegar (5% acidity)

1 quart water

⅔ cup sugar

½ cup Ball® Salt for Pickling &
    Preserving

4 teaspoons crushed red pepper

2 teaspoons pickling spice

7 pounds fresh asparagus

12 dill sprigs

6 garlic cloves, crushed

Ball® Pickle Crisp® Granules
    (optional)

❶ Bring the first 6 ingredients to a boil in a stainless-steel or
enameled saucepan over medium-high, stirring until the sugar
and the salt dissolve.

❷ Rinse the asparagus. Cut the spears into 5-inch lengths to fit the
jars, discarding tough ends. Place 2 dill sprigs and 1 garlic clove into
a hot jar. Tightly pack the asparagus, cut ends down, in jar, leaving
½-inch headspace. Add ⅛ teaspoon Ball® Pickle Crisp® Granules
to jar, if desired. Ladle hot pickling liquid over asparagus, leaving
½-inch headspace. Remove air bubbles. Wipe the jar rim. Center the
lid on the jar. Apply the band, and adjust to fingertip-tight. Place the
jar in the boiling water canner. Repeat until all the jars are filled.

❸ Process the jars 10 minutes, adjusting for altitude. Turn off heat;
remove the lid, and let the jars stand 5 minutes. Remove the jars
and cool.

ZUCCHINI PICKLES

MAKES ABOUT 4 (½-PINT) JARS

Pickling is a tasty way to use a bounty of extra zucchini. The flavor of this pickle is reminiscent of bread and butter pickles.

1 Rinse the zucchini under cold running water; drain. Remove the stems and blossom ends from the zucchini. Cut the zucchini crosswise into ¼-inch slices. Peel the onion. Cut the onion into quarters, and then cut into ¼-inch slices. Combine the zucchini and onion in a large bowl; sprinkle with the salt. Pour cold water over the vegetables just to cover. Let stand 2 hours. Drain the vegetables. Rinse the vegetables under cold running water; drain.

2 Combine the sugar, mustard seeds, celery salt, turmeric, and vinegar in a large stainless-steel or enameled saucepan. Bring the mixture to a boil. Turn off heat. Add the zucchini and onions. Let stand 2 hours. Bring the mixture to a boil. Reduce heat to a simmer; simmer 5 minutes.

3 Pack the hot vegetables into a hot jar, leaving ½-inch headspace. Ladle the hot liquid over the vegetables, leaving ½-inch headspace. Add ⅛ teaspoon Ball® Pickle Crisp® Granules to jar, if desired. Remove air bubbles. Wipe the jar rim. Center the lid on the jar. Apply the band, and adjust to fingertip-tight. Place the jar in the boiling water canner. Repeat until all the jars are filled.

4 Process the jars 15 minutes, adjusting for altitude. Turn off heat; remove the lid, and let the jars stand 5 minutes. Remove the jars and cool.

2 pounds zucchini (about 6 medium)

1 medium onion

¼ cup Ball® Salt for Pickling & Preserving

2 cups sugar

2 teaspoons mustard seeds

1 teaspoon celery salt

1 teaspoon ground turmeric

3 cups vinegar (5% acidity)

Ball® Pickle Crisp® Granules (optional)

HOT PEPPERS

MAKES ABOUT 5 (1-PINT) JARS

**A medley of peppers makes this spicy condiment good to pair
with grilled or roasted meats or to toss in a salad.**

3 pounds hot peppers (such as banana, jalapeño, or serrano peppers)

1 quart plus 2 cups white vinegar (5% acidity)

2 cups water

3 garlic cloves, crushed

Ball® Pickle Crisp® Granules (optional)

1 Rinse the hot peppers under cold running water; drain. Remove the stems and blossom ends from the peppers. Cut the peppers into 1-inch pieces. Place the peppers in a large bowl.

2 Combine the vinegar, water, and garlic in a large stainless-steel or enameled saucepan. Bring the mixture to a boil. Reduce heat to a simmer; simmer 5 minutes. Remove and discard the garlic.

3 Pack the hot peppers into a hot jar, leaving ½-inch headspace. Ladle the hot liquid over the peppers, leaving ½-inch headspace. Add ⅛ teaspoon Ball® Pickle Crisp® Granules to jar, if desired. Remove air bubbles. Wipe the jar rim. Center the lid on the jar. Apply the band, and adjust to fingertip-tight. Place the jar in the boiling water canner. Repeat until all the jars are filled.

4 Process the jars 10 minutes, adjusting for altitude. Turn off heat; remove the lid, and let the jars stand 5 minutes. Remove the jars and cool.

BEET PICKLES

MAKES ABOUT 6 (1-PINT) JARS OR 3 (1-QUART) JARS

Here's another favorite pickle that makes a great addition to salads.

24 small beets (about 8 pounds)

2 cinnamon sticks

1 tablespoon whole allspice

2 cups sugar

1½ teaspoons Ball® Salt for Pickling & Preserving

3½ cups white vinegar (5% acidity)

1½ cups water

Ball® Pickle Crisp® Granules (optional)

1 Rinse the beets under cold running water; drain. Trim the stems and tap roots to 2 inches in length. Boil trimmed, unpeeled beets in water to cover until they give slightly when pierced with a fork. Drain the beets and cool until easy to handle. Peel and chop the beets. Measure 3 quarts chopped beets. Tie the spices in a spice bag or cheesecloth.

2 Combine the spice bag, sugar, salt, vinegar, and water in a large stainless-steel or enameled saucepan. Bring the mixture to a boil, stirring until the sugar and salt dissolve. Reduce heat to a simmer; simmer 15 minutes. Remove and discard the spice bag.

3 Pack the beets into a hot jar, leaving ½-inch headspace. Ladle the hot liquid over the beets, leaving ½-inch headspace. Add ⅛ teaspoon Ball® Pickle Crisp® Granules to the jar, if desired. Remove air bubbles. Wipe the jar rim. Center the lid on the jar. Apply the band, and adjust to fingertip-tight. Place the jar in the boiling water canner. Repeat until all the jars are filled.

4 Process the jars 30 minutes, adjusting for altitude. Turn off heat; remove the lid, and let the jars stand 5 minutes. Remove the jars and cool.

CHANGE IT UP

If you prefer this to be more savory, substitute 3 tablespoons mixed pickling spice or 2 tablespoons caraway seeds and 2 whole black peppercorns for the cinnamon sticks and whole allspice.

WATERMELON RIND PICKLES

MAKES ABOUT 6 (1-PINT) JARS

Indulge in these spiced fruit pickles, which are often impossible to find in today's markets. Serve them with grilled pork or barbecue.

1 Rinse the watermelon under cold running water; pat dry. Cut the watermelon into quarters. Cut each section into 1-inch slices. Remove the dark green peel from the watermelon but do not cut away the white rind; discard the peel. Cut off the pink flesh and reserve for another use. Cut the white watermelon rind into 1-inch cubes to measure 4 quarts. Put 4 quarts of the water in a large stainless-steel or enameled saucepan. Add the salt, stirring until the salt dissolves. Add the cubed watermelon rind. Let stand in the refrigerator 12 hours or overnight. Drain and rinse the watermelon rind under cold running water. Tie the spices in a spice bag or cheesecloth.

2 Combine the watermelon rind and remaining 1 gallon water in a stainless-steel or enameled saucepan. Cook over medium-high until the rind is tender. Drain and set aside. Combine the spice bag, sugar, lemon slices, and vinegar in saucepan. Bring the mixture to a boil, stirring until the sugar dissolves. Reduce heat to a simmer; simmer 10 minutes. Add the watermelon rind. Simmer the watermelon rind until it is transparent. Remove and discard the spice bag.

3 Pack the hot watermelon rind into a hot jar, leaving ½-inch headspace. Ladle the hot pickling liquid over the watermelon rind, leaving ½-inch headspace. Remove air bubbles. Wipe the jar rim. Center the lid on the jar. Apply the band, and adjust to fingertip-tight. Place the jar in the boiling water canner. Repeat until all the jars are filled.

4 Process the jars 10 minutes, adjusting for altitude. Turn off heat; remove the lid, and let the jars stand 5 minutes. Remove the jars and cool.

1 (8-pound) watermelon

8 quarts water

1 cup Ball® Salt for Pickling & Preserving

3 cinnamon sticks

1 tablespoon whole cloves

1 tablespoon whole allspice

¼ teaspoon mustard seeds

7 cups sugar

½ cup thinly sliced lemon (about 1 medium)

2 cups white vinegar (5% acidity)

ASIAN-STYLE CARROT and DAIKON RADISH PICKLES

These Vietnamese-style pickles make a savory garnish for many dishes, including a bánh mì sandwich.

1 Rinse and peel the carrots and radishes, and cut into ⅛-inch julienne strips using a mandoline or knife.

2 Bring 2 cups water and next 3 ingredients to a boil in a 6-quart stainless-steel or enameled Dutch oven, stirring until the salt dissolves; reduce heat, and simmer.

3 Place 1 tablespoon of the coriander seeds, 1 or 2 of the chiles, 2 of the garlic cloves, and one-fourth of the ginger slices into a hot jar. Pack the carrots and radishes tightly into the hot jar, leaving ½-inch headspace.

4 Ladle the hot pickling liquid over the vegetables, leaving ½-inch headspace. Add ⅛ teaspoon Ball® Pickle Crisp® Granules to the jar, if desired. Remove air bubbles. Wipe the jar rim. Center the lid on the jar. Apply the band, and adjust to fingertip-tight. Place the jar in the boiling water canner. Repeat until all the jars are filled.

5 Process the jars 10 minutes, adjusting for altitude. Turn off heat; remove the lid, and let the jars stand 5 minutes. Remove the jars and cool.

1 pound large carrots

¾ pound daikon radishes

2 cups water

2 cups white vinegar (5% acidity)

1 cup sugar

¼ cup Ball® Salt for Pickling & Preserving

¼ cup coriander seeds

4 to 8 small dried red chiles (such as bird's beak peppers or pequín chiles)

8 garlic cloves, crushed

1 (1-inch) piece fresh ginger, peeled and thinly sliced

Ball® Pickle Crisp® Granules (optional)

MEDITERRANEAN REFRIGERATOR PICKLES

MAKES ABOUT 1 (1-QUART) JAR OR 2 (1-PINT) JARS

Classic Mediterranean flavors from oregano or basil and citrus combine in this simple refrigerator pickle. Because they're refrigerated and not preserved for the pantry, you can get a little more creative with the vegetables and seasonings to taste.

2 pounds desired vegetables (see vegetable choices below)

2 cups white vinegar or red wine vinegar (5% acidity), or balsamic vinegar, or a combination

1 cup water

1 tablespoon sugar

1 tablespoon Ball® Salt for Pickling & Preserving

2 tablespoons minced fresh oregano or basil

2 teaspoons citrus zest

¼ teaspoon crushed red pepper

4 garlic cloves, crushed

2 small bay leaves

① Wash, trim, and peel vegetables; leave whole (depending on size), halve, quarter, slice, or chop.

② Bring the vinegar and next 8 ingredients to a boil in a small stainless-steel or enameled saucepan; reduce heat, and simmer 3 minutes, stirring to dissolve sugar and salt.

③ Tightly pack the vegetables into 1 hot (1-quart) or 2 hot (1-pint) jars. Pour the hot brine over the vegetables to cover. Cover jar with lid; let stand 1 hour or until cooled to room temperature. Store in refrigerator for 3 weeks for the best flavor; consume within 3 months. (The longer the pickles stand in the refrigerator, the more flavorful they will become.)

CHANGE IT UP

This recipe works with any combination of the following vegetables: asparagus, button mushrooms, green beans, cauliflower, eggplant, onions, radishes, bell peppers, chile peppers, cherry or grape tomatoes, or zucchini.

PICKLED GINGER

MAKES ABOUT 4 (4-OUNCE) JARS

Keep a jar of this versatile pickle handy in your refrigerator. It works in stir-fries and sauces as a substitution for fresh ginger.

½ pound fresh ginger

1 cup rice vinegar or apple cider vinegar (5% acidity)

6 tablespoons sugar

2 teaspoons Ball® Salt for Pickling & Preserving

1 Peel the ginger, and cut into paper-thin slices.

2 Bring the vinegar, sugar, and salt to a boil in a medium stainless-steel or enameled saucepan, stirring until the sugar and salt dissolve.

3 Firmly pack the ginger slices into a hot jar, leaving ½-inch headspace. Ladle the hot pickling liquid into the jar to cover the ginger, leaving ½-inch headspace. Remove air bubbles. Wipe the jar rim. Center the lid on the jar. Apply the band, and adjust to fingertip-tight. Repeat until all the jars are filled. Cool completely. Chill overnight. Store in the refrigerator up to 3 months. (Pickled Ginger will develop a rosy hue during storage.)

SPICY DILL REFRIGERATOR PICKLES

MAKES ABOUT 1 (1-QUART) JAR OR 2 (1-PINT) JARS

The jalapeño pepper adds just a little kick to classic dill pickles.

1 Rinse, trim, and peel vegetables; leave whole (depending on size), halve, quarter, slice, or chop.

2 Bring the vinegar and next 7 ingredients to a boil in a small stainless-steel or enameled saucepan; reduce heat, and simmer 3 minutes, stirring to dissolve sugar and salt.

3 Tightly pack the vegetables into 1 hot (1-quart) or 2 hot (1-pint) jars. Pour the hot brine over the vegetables to cover. Cover the jar with the lid; let stand 1 hour or until cooled to room temperature. Store in refrigerator for 3 weeks for the best flavor; consume within 3 months. (The longer the pickles stand in the refrigerator, the more flavorful they will become.)

2 pounds desired vegetables (see vegetable choices below)

2 cups white vinegar (5% acidity)

1 cup water

1 tablespoon sugar

1 tablespoon Ball® Salt for Pickling & Preserving

2 teaspoons pickling spice

4 fresh dill sprigs

2 garlic cloves, crushed

1 jalapeño pepper, minced

CHANGE IT UP

This recipe works with any combination of the following vegetables: asparagus, bell peppers, cherry or grape tomatoes, green beans, carrots, cauliflower, pickling cucumbers, green tomatoes, or onions.

PICKLES

SWEET PICKLED RADISH

MAKES ABOUT 1 (1-PINT) JAR

Fresh ruby red radishes with their certain crunch and sharp flavor make delicious and easy refrigerator quick pickles.

1 bunch radishes (about ½ pound), stem and root ends removed and cut into ⅛-inch slices

½ cup white or apple cider vinegar (5% acidity)

½ cup sugar

¼ cup water

1 teaspoon Ball® Salt for Pickling & Preserving

1 teaspoon mustard seeds

½ teaspoon freshly ground black pepper

1 bay leaf

½ teaspoon crushed red pepper (optional)

❶ Rinse the radishes under cold running water; drain. Place the radishes in a hot jar. Bring the vinegar, next 6 ingredients, and, if desired, crushed red pepper to a boil in a small stainless-steel or enameled saucepan, stirring until the sugar and salt dissolve.

❷ Ladle the hot pickling liquid over the radishes, leaving ½-inch headspace. Remove air bubbles. Wipe the jar rim. Center the lid on the jar. Apply the band, and adjust to fingertip-tight. Cool on a wire rack, about 1 hour. Chill 6 hours before serving. Store in the refrigerator up to 3 months.

THE PROBLEM SOLVER

Wondering why your jelly is filled with bubbles or your pickles taste bitter? This problem solver is designed to help you identify the general conditions that may occur in home-canned foods and gives you simple solutions to address them.

The Problem: Jars fail to seal.

Use food immediately, refrigerate immediately, or correct cause and reprocess within 24 hours. To reprocess, remove original lid, empty jars, and reheat food and/or liquid as directed by the recipe. Pack hot food into hot clean jars and cover with a new clean lid. Reprocess refilled jars as in the original recipe.

The Solution:

• Heat process all filled jars using the method and time recommended in the tested recipes for the specific food and jar size. Make sure to adjust processing time for high altitude as required.

• Check for the proper headspace. Use the headspace recommended in the recipe for the specific food and jar size.

• Check for the proper adjustment of lids and bands.

• Check that there are no food particles on the jar rim. Clean the rim using a clean, damp cloth to remove residue before applying the lid.

• Do not invert, move, or shake the jars during the cooling time after processing.

The Problem: Jar seals (or appears to seal) and then unseals.

If spoilage is evident, or you don't know when the jar came unsealed, do not use.

The Solution:

• Heat process all filled jars using the method and time recommended in the tested recipes for the specific food and jar size. Make sure to adjust processing time for high altitude as required.

• Check that there are no food particles on the jar rim. Clean the rim using a clean, damp cloth to remove residue before applying the lid.

• Always use a new lid. They are one-time use only.

• Check that there are no chips or cracks on the jar rim.

• Remove excess air. Leave the recommended headspace when filling the jar and remove the air bubbles to release trapped air before applying lid.

The Problem: Lid buckles, appearing to warp or bulge upward.

If spoilage is evident, do not use food.

The Solution:

• Buckling that occurs immediately after heat processing is caused by an overly tight application of the band. Adjust the band; screw the band downward until fingertip-tight.

• Buckling that occurs during storage is caused by food spoilage. Dispose of the food in a way that prevents consumption by humans or animals.

The Problem: My jam, jelly, or other soft spread won't set.

The Solution:

• The proportions of sugar, juice, or fruit, acid, and pectin are not in balance. Make sure to follow the recipe instructions exactly.

• Fruit used to prepare soft spread is overripe.

• The soft spread is not boiled at a rolling boil for the required length of time. Always bring soft spread to a full rolling boil when using commercial pectin or to 220°F when preparing a recipe with no added pectin.

• The wrong type or amount of pectin was used. Pectin types are not interchangeable. Use only the type of pectin listed in the recipe and measure powdered pectin carefully.

• Some soft spreads may take as long as two weeks before the gel is set. If your jelly or jam won't set after 2 weeks and you followed the recipe instructions completely and accurately, you may remake it in order to achieve a firmer set.

The Problem: My jam, jelly, or other soft spread is tough or stiff.

The Solution:

• This can happen when there's too much natural pectin in the fruit. Make sure the fruit is fully ripe, not under-ripe.

• You may have cooked the jam or jelly too long.

• You may have used too much sugar. Use standard dry measuring cups and level the sugar even with the top edge of the cup.

The Problem: There are bubbles in my spread.

The Solution:

• This is usually caused by not bringing the soft spread to the correct temperature before filling the jars and/or under processing, which prevents spoilage microorganisms such as yeasts from being destroyed. Always bring soft spread to a full rolling boil when using commercial pectin or to 220°F when preparing a recipe with no added pectin.

• If bubbles are stationary when the jar is stationary, air is trapped in the gel. Be sure to ladle the soft spread quickly into the jar, holding the ladle near the rim of the jar or funnel.

The Problem: Fruit floats in soft spread. Mixture gels, but fruit solids and clear jelly separate into layers.

Fruit floating in a sealed jar does not affect the flavor or safety of the food, but may not look as pleasing.

The Solution:

• This can occur when you use immature fruit or porous, textured fruit. Be sure to use fully ripe, freshly picked fruit and berries, either fresh or frozen. Some imported out-of-season fruits are firm textured and tend to float more easily.

• Another cause could be that the sugar content of your soft spread was too high. Be sure to measure carefully and cook the mixture at a full rolling boil for the time indicated in the recipe before filling the jars.

• The cause could also be air in the fruit, which can be dependent on the growing season. There is no solution if this is the case.

The Problem: Food darkens in top of jar.

The Solution:

• Liquid did not cover the food. Completely cover food solids with liquid, making sure headspace is adequate, before applying closures.

• Heat process all filled jars using the method and time recommended in a tested recipe for the specific food and jar size.

• Excess air sealed in the jar due to improper headspace or bubble removal. Use headspace recommended in the recipe and slide a nonmetallic utensil between the food and the jar to release trapped air before applying the lids and screwing on the bands.

• Use the hot pack method when indicated in recipe. Heat process all filled jars using the method and time recommended in a tested fresh preserving recipe for the specific food and jar size.

The Problem: Pickles lack crispness.

The Solution:

• Poor-quality cucumbers may lack crispness. Choose high-quality cucumbers and, if possible, use them within 24 hours of harvest.

• You may have used a variety of cucumber that is not recommended for pickling and canning. Use only pickling cucumbers; other varieties may be good choices for relishes or chutneys.

• This may be due to not using a crisping agent. Use a crisping agent such as Ball® Pickle Crisp® Granules.

The Problem: Pickles are soft or slippery.

The Solution:

• Make sure the blossom ends of the cucumbers are removed. Cut 1/16-inch off blossom ends of the cucumbers. The blossom end contains an enzyme that may cause softening.

• The brine or vinegar may be too weak. Use Ball® Salt for Pickling & Preserving and vinegar with 5% acidity. Follow a current, tested recipe for proper ratios of salt to vinegar.

• The pickles may have been underprocessed and spoilage is occurring. Discard the pickles. In the future, follow the recommended processing time in a current, tested recipe using a boiling water canner.

The Problem: Pickles have a strong, bitter taste.

The Solution:

• This can happen when you use spices that are old, cooked too long in the vinegar, or you used too large a quantity of spice. Use fresh spices— whole spices should be used within 3 to 4 years of purchase. Follow current, tested recipes to ensure that quantities and times are correct.

• You may have used vinegar that was too strong. Always use vinegar at 5% acidity for fresh preserving.

• Using a salt substitute in place of Ball® Salt for Pickling & Preserving could be the problem. Salt substitutes contain potassium chloride, which is naturally bitter.

METRIC EQUIVALENTS

The information in the following charts is provided to help cooks outside the United States successfully use the recipes in this book. All equivalents are approximate.

EQUIVALENTS FOR DIFFERENT TYPES OF INGREDIENTS

Standard Cup	Fine Powder (ex. flour)	Grain (ex. rice)	Granular (ex. sugar)	Liquid Solids (ex. butter)	Liquid (ex. milk)
1	140 g	150 g	190 g	200 g	240 ml
¾	105 g	113 g	143 g	150 g	180 ml
⅔	93 g	100 g	125 g	133 g	160 ml
½	70 g	75 g	95 g	100 g	120 ml
⅓	47 g	50 g	63 g	67 g	80 ml
¼	35 g	38 g	48 g	50 g	60 ml
⅛	18 g	19 g	24 g	25 g	30 ml

LIQUID INGREDIENTS BY VOLUME

¼ tsp =			1 ml
½ tsp =			2 ml
1 tsp =			5 ml
3 tsp = 1 Tbsp =		½ fl oz =	15 ml
2 Tbsp = ⅛ cup =		1 fl oz =	30 ml
4 Tbsp = ¼ cup =		2 fl oz =	60 ml
5⅓ Tbsp= ⅓ cup =		3 fl oz =	80 ml
8 Tbsp = ½ cup =		4 fl oz =	120 ml
10⅔ Tbsp= ⅔ cup =		5 fl oz =	160 ml
12 Tbsp = ¾ cup =		6 fl oz =	180 ml
16 Tbsp = 1 cup =		8 fl oz =	240 ml
1 pt = 2 cups =		16 fl oz =	480 ml
1 qt = 4 cups =		32 fl oz =	960 ml
		33 fl oz =	1000 ml = 1 l

DRY INGREDIENTS BY WEIGHT

(To convert ounces to grams, multiply the number of ounces by 30.)

1 oz	=	1/16 lb	=	30 g
4 oz	=	¼ lb	=	120 g
8 oz	=	½ lb	=	240 g
12 oz	=	¾ lb	=	360 g
16 oz	=	1 lb	=	480 g

LENGTH

(To convert inches to centimeters, multiply the number of inches by 2.5.)

¼ in	=		.5 cm
½ in	=		1.5 cm
1 in	=		2.5 cm
6 in	= ½ ft	=	15 cm
12 in	= 1 ft	=	30 cm

COOKING/OVEN TEMPERATURES

	Fahrenheit	Celsius	Gas Mark
Freeze Water	32° F	0° C	
Room Temperature	68° F	20° C	
Boil Water	212° F	100° C	
Bake	325° F	160° C	3
	350° F	180° C	4
	375° F	190° C	5
	400° F	200° C	6
	425° F	220° C	7
	450° F	230° C	8
Broil			Grill

INDEX